gluten-free *sourdough* baking

The Miracle Method
for Creating Great Bread Without Wheat

mary thompson
Founder of A Couple of Celiacs

PAGE STREET
PUBLISHING CO.

PAGE STREET
PUBLISHING CO.

First published in 2022 by
Page Street Publishing Co.
27 Congress Street, Suite 1511
Salem, MA 01970
www.pagestreetpublishing.com

Distributed by Macmillan, sales in Canada by The Canadian Manda Group.

26 25 24 23   2 3 4 5

ISBN-13: 978-1-64567-524-2
ISBN-10: 1-64567-524-6

Library of Congress Control Number: 2021937942

Cover and book design by Emma Hardy for Page Street Publishing Co.
Photography by Mary Thompson

Printed and bound in the United States

Dedication

This book is dedicated to Patrick and Lucile, my parents, for teaching me so many life skills, and to my two clever and gorgeous girls, Steph and Sam. Love ya!

table of contents

Introduction

When you are on a gluten-free diet, your greatest quest is for really good bread and baked goods. This quest has led me on a fantastic journey of gluten-free sourdough, which is a safe and healthy choice for people with celiac disease, gluten intolerance and other dietary concerns.

I was diagnosed with celiac disease in 2010 after struggling with extreme fatigue. Eating gluten-free at home was not a big hardship for me, but it involved a steep learning curve. I had to educate myself about living gluten-free and understand how glutens like wheat, rye and barley appear not just in bread, but also in sauces and packaged foods of all kinds! I also had to learn to watch for cross contamination at home. I started off with a nutrition class offered at the hospital after I was diagnosed and I did some research online. I also purchased a book called *Gluten-Free Diet: A Comprehensive Resource Guide* by Shelley Case, which I found had the most accurate and detailed information.

Since then, both my daughters have been diagnosed with celiac disease, in addition to some of my other family members in New Zealand, who also inherited it. My eldest daughter and I created a blog, acoupleofceliacs.com, and an Instagram page, @acoupleofceliacs. These outlets allowed us to transform many of our favorite family recipes into gluten-free versions and share them with others. My daughter has since shifted her career into photography; meanwhile, I have fallen head over heels for sourdough.

Sourdough is easier to digest because of its long, slow fermentation process, and I put that advantage to use by making wholesome and nutritious gluten-free sourdough in my own kitchen. Homemade gluten-free sourdough is better for my celiac disease than the highly processed breads I used to eat. I was thrilled to have been given the opportunity to write this cookbook—it allows me to share what I have learned with others so they, too, may enjoy wholesome gluten-free baking.

It still amazes me that it is possible to bake bread with a combination of just flour and water as the leavening agent—and make it entirely gluten-free! When we mix gluten-free flour with water, the starch is broken down into sugar, creating wild yeast and lactic acid that is then transformed into sourdough bread. A sourdough starter, or culture, has the power to raise dough without the use of commercial yeast to create gluten-free bread that is not only visually appealing but also tastes amazing.

Baking sourdough may seem intimidating at first—but once you taste gluten-free sourdough, you will not want to go back to commercial bread, which contains many added starches and gums. You do not need much to start: a kitchen scale, a couple of bowls and a combination of gluten-free flours.

When you bake gluten-free sourdough, you will not experience the dry, fall-apart grittiness often found in other gluten-free breads, because the sourdough fermentation process helps smooth and bind the dough to create the type of baked goods we yearn for. Sourdough is known for its tangy flavor, but with modifications to the temperature and fermentation times, you can produce sweeter doughs to bake impressive gluten-free versions of artisan loaves, buns, crackers, muffins, cakes and more!

Food is a way to connect with others for both physical as well as emotional nourishment. For me, baking—especially with sourdough—has also become a creative outlet. I just love trying new recipes, decorating loaves and experimenting with different flour combinations. The entire process of sourdough is very comforting and satisfying.

I hope this book will inspire you to dive into the gluten-free world of sourdough baking. With this miracle method of making bread, and the simple and consistent steps detailed in these pages, you will soon be enjoying the gluten-free bread you have dreamed about.

After all, the best bread is made in your own kitchen with the ingredients of your choice. It simply does not get any better than that!

Mary

Before You
Get Started

My Gluten–Free Flour Pantry

Gluten is the protein found in wheat, rye and barley, so you will not find those grains here. Gluten provides the stretch and structure needed for baking, so to re-create that missing structure, we need a combination of at least two or three different flours and binding ingredients like psyllium and flaxseed. It is difficult to obtain optimal results with just one type of gluten-free flour, which is why I use multiple kinds of gluten-free flour in every recipe in this book.

If you have already been purchasing gluten-free flour, then you have probably discovered its high cost. Sometimes I go to two or three different stores for a particular gluten-free flour, because each store sells a different selection of flour for a different price. I also look online for sales and buy whole grains to mill, which is definitely more cost-effective. When I consider purchasing a packaged flour blend, I prefer the first one or two ingredients to be whole grains and not starches, due to starch's low nutritional value. For example, Anita's Organic Mill Gluten Free All Purpose Flour specifies oat flour and brown rice flour before some starches in the ingredient list. The best gluten-free flour blends are a combination of heavy to lightweight flours, a starch and a binder. Heavyweight flours include buckwheat, brown rice, teff and nut flours. Medium-weight flours include quinoa, sorghum, oat and millet flours. Lightweight flours include white rice flour and starches. Binders, as I mentioned earlier, include things like psyllium husk and flaxseed. How these items are combined will create different textures, flavors and densities for the finished bake.

Different types of flour absorb water in different ways, and once you are more familiar with the properties of each flour, your sourdough baking will become more intuitive and it will be easier to accomplish spectacular results. You will see how each flour responds to different amounts of water, fermentation time and temperature. Or, if you do not want to worry about these extra details, just follow my recipes, which have been specifically developed to account for each flour's properties.

Gluten-free flours are heavier than wheat flours, so for the best baking results, you should weigh the flours using a kitchen scale. Do not measure the flours by cups. Various companies grind their flours differently, so always find the most finely milled flour so that you can prevent a gritty texture in your baking.

In order to protect yourself from cross contamination with flours containing gluten, with all gluten-free flours, it is best to do some research into where the flour comes from and how it is milled or packaged.

I store most of my flours in sealed jars in a kitchen cupboard because I use them often for baking. If you are not continually using your expensive gluten-free flours, store them in the fridge or freezer and bring them to room temperature before using them. I always store my nut flours and nuts in the fridge to prevent them from turning rancid.

I've compiled a breakdown of all the different types of gluten-free flours used in this book so you can get your gluten-free pantry set up before diving into my recipes.

Brown Rice Flour

Brown rice flour is a heavyweight flour, and although it is a standard in my sourdough starter, I do not often use large amounts of it in my gluten-free baking. It is heavier than white rice flour, with a slightly nuttier flavor. A more finely ground brown rice flour will produce a better baked product, and it will help absorb more water than a coarsely ground flour. There are always variations between brands that can slightly change a recipe. You can substitute a coarsely ground brown rice flour with white rice flour if absolutely necessary, but be sure to adjust the water a little for the right consistency.

Buckwheat Flour

Buckwheat is a seed related to rhubarb, which is why it may sometimes give a pink tinge to the flour when you're growing a gluten-free starter. Buckwheat mills into a heavyweight flour, and despite the name, it does not contain any gluten. It can absorb a lot of moisture—if you use too much of it in a recipe, your baking can become quite wet and sticky or even crumbly. My preference is to buy the hulled buckwheat groats to mill into a lighter-colored flour. It is milder in flavor and I like the light color without the dark flecks from the hull, but this is not a necessity!

Cornstarch

Cornstarch, also known as corn flour where I grew up, is an extremely fine white flour used to lighten the texture of a flour blend.

Corn Flour

Corn flour is also called cornmeal, grits or polenta, and it can be yellow or white in color. I prefer more finely ground flour, but it is possible to grind corn flour further in a food processor if you cannot find the right texture.

Flaxseed

Golden flaxseed is my preference in baking because it looks more attractive in lighter flour blends. The darker-colored flax-seed leaves black specks throughout the baked product. I buy flaxseed whole and grind it in a small electric coffee grinder because it keeps better that way and does not go rancid.

Millet Flour

Millet flour is a whole-grain, medium-weight flour that is yellow in color. It has a mild, sweet flavor. It pairs very well with buckwheat and adds a soft, fluffy texture to baked goods.

Nut and Seed Flours

Flours made from finely ground almonds, hazelnuts, sunflower seeds and pumpkin seeds add the most amazing flavor and texture to gluten-free baking. The oils from the nuts also act as a wonderful binder. You can easily make your own nut flours with raw, certified gluten-free nuts by grinding them into a fine powder in a kitchen blender.

Oat Flour

Oat flour is a medium-weight flour that is gluten-free only if there has been no cross contamination in growing and packaging the oats. Here in Canada, it is easy to find certified gluten-free whole oats and flour. Using too much oat flour can leave your baked goods very wet and dense, but it has excellent binding properties, which is why I like to use it in small amounts. Oats are quick and easy to mill into a fine flour using a food processor. Some people with celiac disease or other dietary restrictions cannot tolerate oats; in that case, you can substitute the oats with buckwheat flour or millet flour. You may need to experiment and add a little more water.

Potato Starch

Potato starch is not the same as potato flour. It is similar in texture and lightness to cornstarch and tapioca starch.

Psyllium Husk

Psyllium husk cannot be substituted with anything else in this book. It is the magic ingredient to bind the flours and give them some stretch and elasticity. Psyllium can be bought whole or in a powdered form. I always use the whole psyllium husk because it is easier to find in my area. I have never used the psyllium powder, and I cannot recommend how much of it to substitute (although I do know you'd use less than you would the whole psyllium husk). Whole psyllium is extremely easy to work with if you immediately mix it into a liquid to prevent clumping. Some people mix psyllium directly into their flour blend, but I have had the best results adding it to a liquid.

Quinoa Flour

Quinoa is a seed that mills into a medium-weight flour to create light and fluffy baked goods. It ferments quickly and is best used in a combination with other flours because it has a strong flavor on its own. Quinoa can be found in many stores in both whole-grain and flour form.

Sorghum Flour

Sorghum is a whole-grain, medium-weight flour with a smooth texture. It is light in color, relatively flavorless and a good base for adding other flours to. You could substitute a portion of sorghum flour with millet flour or oat flour, although oat flour is stickier, so you would need to use less of it.

Sweet White Rice Flour

Sweet white rice flour is a lightweight flour, and there are many names for it, including glutinous (though it does not contain gluten) and sticky white rice flour. It is milled from short-grain rice and has a high starch content. It helps create structure and adds a little extra binding to gluten-free baking, but if you use too much, you will end up with a wet and sticky baked product.

Tapioca Starch

Tapioca starch and tapioca flour are the same thing. It is a medium-weight, starchy white flour with a sweet flavor and is used as a thickener. Tapioca is extracted from the cassava plant and it should not be used on its own, but it is extremely beneficial when it is combined with other flours to lighten their density. Too much tapioca starch will make your baked products thick and gooey. I always buy tapioca starch; I have never milled it.

Teff Flour

Teff is a tiny grain that produces a heavier flour. It is best used in combination with other gluten-free flours, but too much of it can produce dry baked goods. It has a strong flavor. Teff flour is often dark brown in color, but you can also find a light-colored grain.

White Rice Flour

White rice flour is a lightweight flour that gives fluffiness to a flour blend, and it is my preferred flour for dusting a banneton. You could substitute white rice flour for brown rice flour and increase the water a little. White rice flour will ferment more quickly than brown rice flour.

Milling Your Own Flour

There are many good reasons to mill your own flour. Freshly milled flour tastes better. It still contains the germ, bran and fresh oils that have not gone rancid, and it is higher in nutrients. You can mill exactly what you need, and it is quick and easy to do. You control how fine or coarse your flour is, which is important. Freshly milled flour is lighter in weight because it has not had time to compact, which results in a lighter baked product. You can blend your own flours to get exactly the flavor and texture of bread that you want, and it is cheaper to buy gluten-free whole grains than already milled flour.

When you mill your own flour, it gives you the opportunity to source the best quality gluten-free grains. There are some flours that are far cheaper to make at home and, after having a mill in my kitchen for the past year and a half, I would not trade it for anything. My mill is a KoMo Fidibus Classic; it has a 360-watt motor, and it has the capability to grind from coarse to fine just by rotating the hopper. This mill will grind dry grains like oats, millet, corn, teff, quinoa, rice and much more. Some spices and seeds, such as flaxseed, are detrimental to the grinding stones because of their oils, so I grind spices and seeds in a small electric coffee grinder instead.

In all the recipes in this cookbook, I have used unsifted flour that I have milled from whole grains myself and also unsifted flour straight from a package, meaning there are no weight adjustments necessary if you do the same.

How to Cultivate and Maintain a Gluten-Free Sourdough Starter

A gluten-free sourdough starter is required for making gluten-free sourdough bread. A starter is just the natural fermentation of flour and water that occurs when the flour-water mixture is left on the counter—and it creates flavorful and amazing bread. I prefer to use good-quality whole grains to grow a strong gluten-free starter. All the recipes in this book are made with a buckwheat flour and brown rice flour starter.

Here are the supplies you'll need to create your own gluten-free sourdough starter:

- 2 (500- to 750-ml) clean jars (such as WECK brand jars with glass lids)
- Brown rice flour
- Buckwheat flour
- Filtered or unchlorinated warm water
- Kitchen scale (a must-have for accuracy)
- Dedicated starter spoon—such as a small wooden spoon—that is always clean and free from food contaminants to prevent unwanted mold or bacteria

Tips for Success

Make sure to keep the jar covered with a loose-fitting lid or cloth and a rubber band.

Place the jar in a warm place—for example, in a bread proofer, in the oven with the light off or on top of the fridge—to keep it at a consistent temperature of 69 to 82°F (21 to 28°C) for 24 hours.

If your house is cool, you can leave the starter in your oven with the light turned on. It is advisable to leave a large note on the oven door that reads "Don't turn on the oven."

I find it is easiest to feed my starter at breakfast and dinnertime, but make sure to set up the schedule that is most convenient for you.

Day 1, morning: In a clean 500- to 750-millilter jar, mix 20 grams of brown rice flour, 20 grams of buckwheat flour and 50 grams of warm water, using the kitchen scale to measure the ingredients precisely. Using the dedicated starter spoon, mix the ingredients well to make sure there is no loose flour. Adjust the amount of water if your starter is too dry (it will be very stiff and hard to stir, like a thick batter) or the amount of flour if your starter is too runny (it will be like a thin pancake batter). You may need to make these adjustments due to variations in flour milled from different companies. The consistency of the starter should be easy to stir but not pourable, and it should stick to the sides of the jar.

Cover the jar and leave it in a warm place.

Day 1, evening: Add 50 grams of warm water to the morning's starter and vigorously mix the starter to aerate it a little. Add 20 grams of brown rice flour and 20 grams of buckwheat flour. Mix the ingredients well to make sure there is no loose flour. Cover the jar and leave it in a warm place.

Day 2, morning: Add 50 grams of warm water to the starter from day 1 and vigorously mix the starter to aerate it a little. Add 20 grams of brown rice flour and 20 grams of buckwheat flour. Mix the ingredients well to make sure there is no loose flour. Cover the jar and leave it in a warm place. You may start to see some activity and bubbles—but that does not always happen at this stage, so don't worry if you don't see any activity. There is no discarding until day 3 and you see some activity in the form of small bubbles, a spongy texture, an increase in size and a sweeter doughy smell.

Day 2, evening: Add 50 grams of warm water to the morning's starter and vigorously mix the starter to aerate it a little. Add 20 grams of brown rice flour and 20 grams of buckwheat flour. Mix the ingredients well to make sure there is no loose flour. Cover the jar and leave it in a warm place.

Day 3, morning and evening: Start to discard some of your starter if it is active, with small bubbles, a foamy texture and an increase in size by at least 30 percent. Otherwise, follow the same routine of feeding from day 1 and day 2 for another day until you see activity. Remember to keep the starter warm at a consistent temperature of between 69 to 82°F (21 to 28°C). My sourdough does very well at a room temperature of 72°F (22°C).

Transfer 40 grams of the starter to a clean jar, then whisk in 50 grams of warm water, 20 grams of brown rice flour and 20 grams of buckwheat flour.

Place the starter discard into its own jar and keep it in the fridge. Add starter discard to this same jar with each discard. Start to discard some of the starter at every feeding, twice a day. With the discarded starter, you can make pizza, pancakes, crackers, cakes and more. See the chapter titled "Leftover Sourdough Starter Treats" (page 155) for some great ways to use up this discarded starter.

Day 4 through day 7, or a few days more: Continue the same discarding and feeding schedule as day 3, twice a day, until the starter has grown by 30 to 50 percent and is bubbly with a mild yeasty smell between each feeding. It may take anywhere from 4 to 8 hours for the starter to become bubbly, depending on the temperature. Around day 3 or 4, it is normal to see your starter do nothing, but it will begin to bubble away with consistent feeding and warm temperatures.

Day 7 through day 10: Due to temperature and the fermenting time for different flours, the readiness of your starter to be used for baking can vary; for example, quinoa flour ferments faster than buckwheat or brown rice flour. You are ready to bake when your starter shows these signs:

·   You begin to see a regular rise and fall after being fed.
·   It peaks and has a nice dome.
·   The texture is light and spongy.
·   The aroma is a little like yogurt.
·   You can see and hear bubbles popping.

Sourdough Starter Tips

Feed the starter around your schedule—breakfast and dinner-time are easy to remember.

Keep the starter out of direct sunlight and in a warm place.

Do not let your starter grow too warm (90°F [32°C]) or too cold (64°F [18°C]).

After the starter is established and active, you do not need to use large amounts of flour to feed it. This will reduce your costs, because gluten-free flour is expensive. I often feed just 25 grams of starter to maintain it when I am not baking.

Once your starter is active—after it has been fermenting for 7 to 10 days and is at the baking stage—you can leave your starter in the fridge for up to 1 week when you are not baking. You can leave your starter in an airtight jar for 2 to 3 weeks if you are away from home, but it will take longer to become active again, and it can also be dehydrated for a longer storage time. Reactivate the starter by bringing it to room temperature and feeding it two or three times before baking with it.

If the starter has fallen a little after peaking, you can still mix it into your dough. If you wait much longer, then you will not get a good rise from your bread. If the starter has peaked (that is,

if it has domed like the top of a balloon and has risen) 4 to 8 hours after being fed, then it will start to fall (that is, the top will become concave or flat and it will have less height). If it has been more than an hour since the starter peaked, then I recommend feeding it again before baking with it.

If you do not like the smell of the sourdough starter, you may not like the taste in your bread either. Discard some starter and feed it again before using it. You can also take a small taste of your starter to check the flavor before using it.

If there is liquid—known as hooch—on top, just pour it off and feed your starter.

Liquid on top and a vinegary smell are signs that your starter needs feeding.

Most important of all, just be patient—you cannot rush sourdough!

Building a Levain to Bake Bread

A levain (also known as a leaven, culture, pre-ferment or mother) is just a separate piece of the starter. Both the starter and levain are fed and left to ferment, and your levain is basically just a second feeding from your starter. You never use all of the starter to build a levain because you need leftover starter for the main culture and future bakes. The starter is fed, and then about 8 hours later, a portion of the starter is fed to build the levain, which is added directly to the dough to bake the bread. The levain is what will give your bread its rise, and it replaces commercial yeast.

There are many ways and ratios that can be used to build a levain, but I most often work with a 1:2:2 ratio (starter: water: flour). For example, to make a total of 150 grams of levain, you will need to perform this equation: $150 \div 5$ (i.e., $1 + 2 + 2$) = 30. Therefore, you will need 30 grams of starter, 60 grams of water and 60 grams of flour. Once your starter shows all the promising signs of activity and it doubles or nearly doubles in size, you are ready to mix some dough.

Sourdough Baking Tools

There are tools for making sourdough that are nice to have, and they will make your baking life easier. Then, there are some tools you absolutely need. You will get exceptionally better results from using a Dutch oven to bake your rustic loaves, a pizza stone to bake fougasse or pizza and loaf pans to hold the shape of the quick breads. Following are the tools used for the recipes in this book.

Essential Tools

Dutch oven: Use a Dutch oven to steam the bread and create a deliciously crusty loaf. You can also use a cast-iron skillet, a pizza stone or a loaf pan if it will handle a temperature of 450°F (232°C). Here are the dimensions I recommend: 11 inches (28 cm) in diameter by 4 inches (10 cm) deep.

Jars: You need two 500- to 750-ml clean starter jars with loose-fitting lids or a piece of cloth with a rubber band. I like to use WECK brand jars with glass lids.

Kitchen scale: You need a scale to weigh gluten-free flour. It is necessary to achieve accurate results, and measuring by cups is too inaccurate. Each person measures flour a little differently, leading to varied results that do not always work

for the final baked product. There are many inexpensive scales to be found both in stores and online.

Loaf pan: Following are the two pans used for the recipes in this book:

- Emile Henry Bread Loaf Baker with lid measuring 11 x 5 x 4.7 inches (28 x 13 x 12 cm)
- Jamie Oliver deep loaf pan (1.5 L) measuring 8 x 5 x 4 inches (20 x 13 x 10 cm)

Oven mitts: You need a good pair of heavy-duty oven mitts to safely handle the extreme heat of a Dutch oven.

Parchment paper: I use a good-quality nonstick parchment paper from Costco that is oven-safe to 425°F (218°C), and I have used it in temperatures up to 500°F (260°C) with no burning.

Pie plate: An Emile Henry 9-inch (23-cm) round ceramic pie plate can be used not only for baking pies but also quiches, pizzas and other gluten-free dishes.

Proofing bowl: A 4-cup (1-L) glass kitchen storage bowl with a lid works well.

Small spoon: You need a dedicated sourdough spoon to avoid any unwanted contaminants. I prefer a wooden spoon, but stainless steel is also okay to use.

Nice-to-Have Tools

Bench scraper: This is a broad, rectangular blade with a sharp edge on one side and a handle on the other side. Gluten-free doughs are often sticky, and a scraper is great for cleaning work surfaces, bowls and your hands. It is a handy tool to help you scoop up the dough and place it in a banneton, or you can use it like a knife to cut dough.

Banneton, brotform or proofing basket: These are all baskets that can be used to proof bread dough. You need a basket to proof the dough in, but you can also use a kitchen bowl lined with a tea towel to give your dough the final shape. Gluten-free doughs will spread too much in a large, wide banneton. You need a smaller basket with tall sides for the best results and crumb. Here are the bannetons I recommend:

- Round banneton 7 inches (18 cm) in diameter by 3½ inches (9 cm) deep

- Oval banneton 11 inches (28 cm) long by 6 inches (15 cm) wide by 3 inches (8 cm) deep

Bread cloche: A cloche creates a steamed environment like a Dutch oven does to create a crispy crust and a soft interior. The base is flat with a domed lid that sits on top. The base can be used as a pizza stone as well. Here is the one I recommend:

- Emile Henry brand ceramic cloche 13 inches (33 cm) in diameter by 7 inches (18 cm) high

Bread lame, razor blade or small knife: Use this to score your bread and create designs.

Bread proofer: A bread proofer is not a necessity, but if you are going to bake sourdough on a regular basis, I highly recommend purchasing one. It is amazing for cooler weather, as it will give you a consistent rise from your sourdough every time. The bread proofer I use is from Brod & Taylor® and it folds flat in order to fit into a large drawer. Use the oven with only the light on as an alternative.

English Muffin rings: I recommend keeping ten 3½-inch (9-cm) rings on hand.

Grain mill: On my kitchen counter, I have a KoMo Fidibus Classic grain mill to make my own gluten-free flour. A mill is not a necessity, but it does pay for itself over time if you do a lot of baking, and it can create many different flours that you cannot always find in stores. (See page 11 for more information about milling your own flour.)

Tart pan: I use an 8 x 5 x 4–inch (20 x 13 x 10–cm) rectangular pan to make the Sourdough Quiche (page 151), but a pie plate or a shallow casserole dish could also be used for the recipe.

Thermometer: A thermometer makes it easy to check the temperature of water and dough for optimal dough growth.

Seasoning a New Banneton

Before baking with a new banneton, you need to prepare it for baking—a process that is commonly referred to as seasoning. I use cane bannetons that now have a permanent coating of flour to prevent the dough from sticking to the basket. It is important that your dough rises and leaves the banneton easily before baking!

When preparing a banneton for its first use, wipe the banneton with a damp cloth and let it partially dry before dusting it with white rice flour. Shake out the excess flour, but make sure a thin layer of flour remains, sticking to the cane.

Flour will build up in the cracks and every so often you can brush this out, or you can even rinse the basket and leave it in the sun to dry before recoating it with flour. It is not recommended to wash a banneton but to just shake out the loose flour and dust it with new flour before each use.

Cover your banneton with a tea towel or store it upside down in a cupboard. Mine sits on top of my fridge.

Vegan Substitutions

Food allergies, sensitivities and plant-based preferences create the need for delicious and nutritious recipes that are not only gluten-free but also dairy-free and vegan. Cooking gluten-free and vegan can be a little daunting, but the recipes in this book have you covered—it is easy to do both. By switching some of the ingredients with your favorite vegan substitutes, you will still be able to eat the best bread! Be aware that a few of my recipes—like the Cheese and Beer Bread (page 60), Braided Herb and Cheese Loaf (page 102), Sourdough Quiche (page 151) and Carrot Tortillas (page 156)—may not work as well with these vegan ingredients, so I suggest sticking to the original ingredients for those recipes.

Vegan Substitutions

Traditional Ingredient	Vegan Ingredient	Notes
1 medium egg (for baking)	45 grams aquafaba plus 1 gram whole psyllium husk	Aquafaba is the cooking water from white beans, usually chickpeas. You can use aquafaba from homemade or canned beans.
1 medium egg (for egg wash)	Olive oil or coconut oil	Lightly brush the dough with oil as you would an egg wash and keep an eye on the dough as it bakes to check for overbrowning.
Butter	Gluten-free vegan butter	Many brands of vegan butter exist on the market. Different types may slightly affect the consistency of the dough, but the final results should be very close to those obtained by using dairy butter.
Cream cheese	Gluten-free vegan cream cheese	Different types of vegan cream cheese may slightly affect the consistency of the dough, but the final results should be very close to those obtained by using dairy cream cheese.
Meat	Gluten-free vegan meat	There are numerous types and brands of vegan meats, but many contain gluten, so be sure to read ingredient lists carefully. You can also use less-processed sources of protein, such as tofu, tempeh and legumes.
Milk	Gluten-free vegan milk	The consistency of oat milk creates the best results with these recipes. Different brands and types of vegan milk may affect the consistency of the dough, but the final results should be very close to those obtained by using dairy milk.
Sour cream	Gluten-free vegan sour cream	There are many brands of vegan sour cream that use cashew nuts, tofu and other plant-based ingredients. Different types may slightly affect the consistency of the dough, but the final results should be very close to those obtained by using dairy sour cream.
Yogurt	Gluten-free vegan yogurt	Many brands of vegan yogurt exist on the market. Different types may slightly affect the consistency of the dough, but the final results should be very close to those obtained by using dairy yogurt.

artisan loaves

If you have celiac disease or must eliminate gluten from your life for any other reason, it takes a certain amount of creativity to enjoy a varied diet, especially when it comes to bread! Home-baked sourdough loaves like the ones in this chapter allow you to once again eat all those favorites that you were missing. There is nothing like a slice of fresh bread!

This chapter is the ideal place to make your first loaf of freshly baked gluten-free sourdough. Once your starter is bubbly and active and you have all the supplies I list for your gluten-free sourdough baking (page 15), you are ready to begin. The Beginner Loaf (page 20) is a great starting point, but if you are new to the world of sourdough, I recommend you make this bread a few times before moving on to other beginner loaves like the Classic Loaf (page 27) or the Rustic Honey and Oat Loaf (page 30). Doing so will help you gain a better understanding of the temperature and timing, which require a bit of practice.

The Beginner *Loaf*

This is a great loaf with which to begin your gluten-free sourdough journey. I hope you become as hooked on the whole process as I am! Everything you could possibly need to know about making gluten-free sourdough is in this recipe, and it is perfect for beginners as a great reference point for the materials, tips and tricks, and schedule detailed here. By following this proven, step-by-step recipe, you can make your sourdough dance to your tune and not the other way around, with little effort needed.

This is a very versatile bread that complements the topping you add to your toast or the filling in your sandwich. There are no eggs, oil, corn, oats or dairy to suit many dietary restrictions, and you can add extra flavor by adding herbs or seeds.

One thing to note: Gluten-free dough can proof very quickly, so this is a good reason to mix it up the night before baking and leave it in the fridge overnight.

―✦―

Makes 1 loaf

Supplies

Active starter (see page 12)

Kitchen scale

1 (500- to 750-ml) jar for the levain

Seasoned banneton (see page 16) or a bowl and a tea towel

Bench scraper

Reusable plastic bag, to cover the dough

Dutch oven, oven-safe pot with a lid, cast-iron skillet or loaf pan

Parchment paper

Bread lame, small knife or razor blade, for scoring

Levain

50 g active starter

100 g warm water

50 g buckwheat flour

50 g brown rice flour

Reactivate your starter the day before you plan on building the levain. A good time to do this is when you get up in the morning, to allow the starter 6 to 8 hours to become bubbly and active. You will need 50 grams of starter for the levain and at least 20 grams left over for maintaining your original starter/main culture. This is a 1:2:2 feeding ratio (see page 14 for more information on the feeding ratio).

Note that if the starter is not active enough, you may need to feed it again and use it before it goes past its peak and begins to fall. This could be between 6 and 8 hours, depending on the temperature in your kitchen. The starter will look spongy and have a dome on the top when it is at its peak. You should refeed your starter before building the levain if it begins to decrease in height, if it has a flat top and if more than an hour has gone by since it began falling. The starter does not need to double in size, but it does need to increase by about 30 percent, smell doughy and have bubbles!

Build the levain: Using the kitchen scale, weigh 50 grams of active starter in a clean jar. Add 100 grams of warm water and vigorously whisk the starter and water together. Add 50 grams of buckwheat flour and 50 grams of brown rice flour. Ferment the levain for 6 to 8 hours, or until it is bubbly and has risen to a peak. Then, mix it into the dough (see the timeline on page 25).

(continued)

Note .... I have found that my loaves have better oven spring (i.e., rise) if my levain is still rising and has not gone past its peak and fallen—just like the starter.

Reactivate the starter.

Combine the flour.

Stir in the psyllium husk.

Mix the dough.

Ferment the dough in a covered bowl.

Knead the dough.

Shape the dough.

Place the dough into the banneton.

Proof the dough.

The Beginner Loaf (continued)

Loaf

70 g sorghum flour

70 g buckwheat flour

60 g brown rice flour

30 g raw unsalted pumpkin seeds, finely ground

75 g tapioca starch

8 g salt

350 g water at 80 to 93°F (27 to 34°C)

30 g pure maple syrup, at room temperature

20 g whole psyllium husk

White rice flour, as needed

Mix the dough: In a large bowl, combine the sorghum flour, buckwheat flour, brown rice flour, pumpkin seeds, tapioca starch and salt. In a medium bowl, combine the warm water and maple syrup. Stir in the psyllium husk to form a gel. Immediately whisk the psyllium gel to prevent lumps from forming, then whisk in the levain and add this gel-levain mixture to the flour blend. Mix the dough well by hand, or with a kitchen mixer fitted with a dough hook running at medium-low speed, until all the ingredients are fully incorporated.

Ferment: Form the dough into a ball, and then place it in a 4-cup (1-L) proofing bowl. Cover the bowl with its lid, and then transfer the bowl to the cold oven with the light on. Let the dough rest in the oven for 30 to 60 minutes, or until the dough begins to rise a little. You do not want the dough to rise too much yet because you need to save most of the dough's rise for the proofing stage. Place the dough, still in the covered bowl, in the fridge for the night.

Shape: The next day, remove the dough from the fridge and leave it at room temperature for about 30 minutes, until it is warm enough to work with. Liberally dust a 7-inch (18-cm) round banneton with the white rice flour. If you do not have a banneton, you can place a clean tea towel in a bowl and generously dust it with white rice flour.

Lightly dampen a work surface with water. Transfer the dough to the prepared work surface and, with wet hands, press the heel of your hand into the dough, pressing down and away from you, then fold the dough over and rotate it. Sprinkle a little white rice flour on the dough's surface, then repeat the kneading process for about 1 minute. With cupped hands, drag the dough in small circles to shape it into a smooth ball. Pinch, seal and smooth any seams in the dough. Scoop the dough up with a bench scraper and gently place it seam side up in the prepared banneton.

Proof: Place the dough, still in the banneton, inside a reusable plastic bag and let it rest at room temperature—ideally about 72°F (22°C)—for 3 to 5 hours. The proofing time depends on the temperature of your kitchen. If the temperature is a little colder, place the dough in the cold oven with just the light on. In the summer warmth, the dough can be left on the counter, and it may benefit from less proofing time. When the dough has proofed enough, it should have risen and should feel soft, puffy and spongy on the sides and in the center. Do not overproof the dough or there will be no rise left for the oven. If you are uncertain, bake the bread sooner rather than later. Chill the dough, still in the banneton, for 30 minutes to prevent the dough from spreading too much in the oven and to make it easier to score.

(continued)

Remove the banneton from the dough.   *Score and bake the dough.*   *Cool the bread.*

Note ·············· If you forget to remove the Dutch oven's lid and reduce the oven's temperature, you will have a burnt and over-cooked loaf. If your oven is extra hot, you can place a baking sheet on the bottom rack of the oven to prevent your bread from burning underneath.

Score: Preheat the oven to 450°F (232°C) with a Dutch oven inside. Meanwhile, cut out some parchment paper and place it on top of the dough in the banneton. Place a small cutting board on top of the parchment paper and gently flip the banneton over. The cutting board will now be on the bottom. Remove the banneton from the dough and gently dampen the surface of the dough with wet fingers. Sift some white rice flour onto the wet dough, then evenly spread the flour, covering all the dough's surface with your hands and score a pattern on the top with a bread lame.

To bake in a Dutch oven: Gently slide the parchment paper with the dough into the Dutch oven, being incredibly careful not to burn yourself. Cover the Dutch oven and bake the bread for 25 minutes to steam the loaf—this stage is when you will see the rise (i.e., the oven spring). Reduce the oven's temperature to 400°F (204°C), remove the Dutch oven's lid to allow the loaf to brown and bake for 30 to 35 minutes. The bread is done when it has turned golden brown, feels firm to the touch and contains no soft areas. When you tap on the bottom of your loaf after letting it cool slightly, a hollow sound will also indicate that the loaf is cooked.

To bake in a loaf pan: Bake the bread at 450°F (232°C) for 35 minutes, then reduce the oven's temperature to 400°F (204°C) and bake the bread for 30 to 35 minutes.

Place the hot sourdough on a wire rack to cool for at least 2 hours before slicing it. Otherwise, you will end up with a gummy loaf that will quickly dry out.

Sourdough keeps well on the kitchen counter, covered, for 2 to 3 days, but after that it is best to slice the remainder and freeze it. The sourdough will last in the freezer for up to 3 months.

Suggested Timeline

Day 1

8:30 a.m.: Feed the starter sometime between 6:30 a.m. and 8:30 a.m.

2:30 p.m.: Build the levain in a jar and place it in a bread proofer or in the oven with the light on to rest for 6 to 8 hours.

8:30 p.m.: Mix the dough and place it into a 4-cup (1-L) proofing bowl. Put the lid on the bowl, and then place the bowl in the oven with the light on. Let the dough rest for 30 to 60 minutes, or until the dough begins to rise a little.

9:30 p.m.: Place the dough, still in the covered bowl, in the fridge for the night.

Day 2

7:30 a.m.: The next day, remove the dough from the fridge and rest it at room temperature to warm up.

8:30 a.m.: Knead, shape and place the dough in a proofing bowl or banneton for the final rise.

1:30 p.m.: Chill the dough, still in the banneton, in the fridge for 30 minutes.

2:00 p.m.: Preheat the oven (with the Dutch oven inside) and score a pattern on the dough.

2:30 p.m.: Bake your loaf of bread and allow it to cool for 2 to 3 hours before slicing it.

Classic *Loaf*

Here is a gluten-free version of a sourdough classic. Enjoy a slice of this beautiful sourdough, with its crispy crust and soft, light interior. This is a perfect recipe to make after you have mastered The Beginner Loaf (page 20). There are many ways to make sourdough, and this recipe will show you a different technique, which has three levain feedings and requires starter to be fed the night before. The dough grows to a great size because it is constantly being fed and the gluten-free flours ferment quickly. There is also a larger percentage of levain in the dough, which causes it to ferment and rise more quickly. This bread always looks impressive coming out of the oven. It is a slightly larger loaf of bread that does equally well in a loaf pan, shaped as a boule (i.e., a round shape) or a bâtard (i.e., an oval shape).

Makes 1 loaf

Morning Levain Feeding
(after the levain has risen to a peak, add the whole amount to the afternoon feeding)

25 g active starter

30 g warm water

15 g brown rice flour

15 g buckwheat flour

Afternoon Levain Feeding
(after the levain has risen to a peak, add the whole amount to the evening feeding)

85 g levain from the morning feeding

55 g warm water

25 g brown rice flour

25 g buckwheat flour

Evening Levain Feeding

190 g levain from morning and afternoon feedings

120 g warm water

50 g brown rice flour

50 g buckwheat flour

Reactivate your starter the day before you plan on building the levain. A good time to do this is right before bed, to allow the starter 6 to 8 hours to become bubbly and active. You will need 25 grams for the levain and at least 20 grams left over for maintaining your original starter/main culture (see page 14 for more information on the feeding ratio).

Build the levain: This is done in three stages. For the morning levain feeding, use a kitchen scale to weigh 25 grams of active starter in a clean 500-milliliter jar. Add 30 grams of warm water, 15 grams of brown rice flour and 15 grams of buckwheat flour, for a total weight of 85 grams. Mix the ingredients well.

For the afternoon levain feeding, put the 85 grams of levain from the morning levain feeding in a clean 750-milliliter jar and add 55 grams of warm water, 25 grams of brown rice flour and 25 grams of buckwheat flour, for a total weight of 190 grams. Mix the ingredients well.

For the evening levain feeding, late in the evening, put 190 grams of levain from the previous two feedings in a 4-cup (1-L) proofing bowl. Add 120 grams of warm water, 50 grams of brown rice flour and 50 grams of buckwheat flour, for a total weight of 410 grams. Mix the ingredients well, cover the levain in the bowl with the bowl's lid and leave it overnight to ferment for 8 to 10 hours.

(continued)

The Classic *Loaf* (continued)

Loaf

95 g sorghum flour

60 g oat flour

40 g millet flour

30 g buckwheat flour

65 g tapioca starch

20 g brown rice flour

7 g salt

30 g finely ground pumpkin seeds

15 g finely ground sunflower seeds

330 g warm water

15 g olive oil

15 g golden syrup or pure maple syrup

15 g brown sugar

12 g ground flaxseed

14 g whole psyllium husk

1 tsp caraway seeds or seeds of choice

White rice flour, as needed

Mix the dough: In a large bowl, weigh the sorghum flour, oat flour, millet flour, buckwheat flour, tapioca starch, brown rice flour, salt, pumpkin seeds and sunflower seeds. In a medium bowl, combine the warm water, olive oil, golden syrup and brown sugar. Stir in the flaxseed and psyllium husk to form a gel. Immediately whisk the psyllium gel to prevent lumps from forming, then whisk in the levain and caraway seeds. Add this gel-levain mixture to the flour blend. Mix the dough well by hand, or with a kitchen mixer fitted with a dough hook running at medium-low speed, until all the ingredients are fully incorporated.

Ferment: Form the dough into a ball, then place it in a 4-cup (1-L) proofing bowl. Cover the bowl with its lid and place the bowl in the oven with the light on. Let the dough rest for 30 to 60 minutes, or until the dough begins to rise a little. Place the covered bowl in the fridge overnight for the bulk fermentation.

Shape: The next day, remove the dough from the fridge and leave it at room temperature for about 30 minutes, until it is warm enough to work with. Liberally dust a 7-inch (18-cm) round banneton with the white rice flour. Lightly dampen a work surface with water. Transfer the dough to the prepared work surface. Knead the dough with wet hands for 2 to 3 minutes, and then shape it into a ball. Sprinkle a little white rice flour on the dough's surface, then repeat the kneading process for about 1 minute. With cupped hands, drag the dough in small circles to shape it into a smooth ball. Pinch, seal and smooth any seams in the dough. Scoop the dough up with a bench scraper and gently place it seam side up in the prepared banneton. To bake this bread in a loaf pan, line the pan with parchment paper, leaving overhanging "handles" of parchment paper on each side of the pan. After shaping the dough into a ball, roll it with the palm of your hand a few times to create an oval shape, and then place it in the prepared loaf pan.

Proof: Place the dough, still in the banneton or loaf pan, inside a reusable plastic bag and let it rest at room temperature—ideally about 72°F (22°C)—for 3 to 5 hours. The proofing time depends on the temperature of your kitchen. If the temperature is a little colder, place the dough in the oven with the light on. In the summer warmth, the dough can be left on the counter, and it may benefit from less proofing time. When the dough has proofed enough, it will have risen and will feel soft, puffy and spongy on the sides and in the center.

Score: If you will be baking the bread in a Dutch oven, preheat the oven to 450°F (232°C) with a Dutch oven inside. Meanwhile, cut out some parchment paper for the dough to sit on. Place the parchment paper on top of the dough, which should still be in the banneton. Flip the banneton upside down, so that the parchment paper is underneath to hold the dough, and remove the banneton. If baking in a loaf pan, leave the dough in the pan. Lightly dampen the surface of the dough with wet fingers. Sprinkle some white rice flour on the dough, then evenly spread the flour around the top of the dough with your hands. Score a design on top of the dough.

To bake in a Dutch oven: Gently slide the parchment paper with the dough into the Dutch oven. Cover the Dutch oven and bake the bread for 25 minutes. Remove the Dutch oven's lid, reduce the oven's temperature to 400°F (204°C) and bake the loaf for 35 minutes. Reduce the oven's temperature to 350°F (177°C) and remove the loaf from the Dutch oven. Place the loaf on the oven's center rack and bake it for 10 minutes, or until the loaf feels firm.

To bake in a loaf pan: Preheat the oven to 450°F (232°C). Bake the loaf for 35 minutes, then reduce the oven's temperature to 400°F (204°C) and bake the loaf for 30 to 35 minutes. Remove the loaf from the pan. If the loaf is soft and undercooked on the bottom, place it directly on the oven's middle rack and bake it for 10 minutes at 350°F (177°C).

Place the hot sourdough on a wire rack to cool for at least 2 hours before slicing it.

Wrap the bread in a tea towel or beeswax wraps and store it on the counter for 2 to 3 days. If your sourdough begins to dry out too quickly, it is best to slice and freeze the remainder. The sourdough will last in the freezer for up to 3 months.

Rustic Honey *and* Oat Loaf

Creamy gluten-free oats added to scrumptious honey-sweetened bread yields a beautiful honey color and a wonderful texture to this loaf. Is there anything better than a thick slice of bread with butter and honey alongside a hot cup of tea? A toasted slice of this bread in the morning makes a quick and easy breakfast.

Note: With the addition of cooked oats mixed into the dough, this recipe may need a little extra baking time. Tap on the bottom of the loaf after baking it—if the bread does not sound hollow or it feels too soft, bake it for 5 to 10 minutes longer.

Makes 1 loaf

Levain

30 g active starter

60 g warm water

30 g buckwheat flour

30 g brown rice flour

Loaf

20 g whole gluten-free oats

60 g cold milk

70 g sorghum flour

65 g tapioca starch

30 g millet flour

30 g buckwheat flour

30 g brown rice flour

9 g salt

280 g warm water

50 g honey

12 g molasses

23 g whole psyllium husk

White rice flour, as needed

Reactivate your starter the day before you plan on building the levain. A good time to do this is when you get up in the morning, to allow the starter 6 to 8 hours to become bubbly and active. You will need 30 grams for the levain and at least 20 grams for maintaining your original starter/main culture (see page 14 for more information on the feeding ratio).

Build the levain: Weigh 30 grams of active starter in a clean 500-milliliter jar, then add 60 grams of warm water and vigorously whisk the ingredients together. Add the 30 grams of buckwheat flour and the 30 grams of brown rice flour. Ferment the levain for 6 to 8 hours, or until it is bubbling and it has risen to a peak, before mixing it into the dough.

Mix the dough: In a medium saucepan, combine the oats and cold milk. Cook the oats over medium-low heat for 3 to 4 minutes, stirring them occasionally, until they have absorbed all the milk. Set the oats aside to cool for about 10 minutes, or until they are not hot to the touch. In a large bowl, combine the sorghum flour, tapioca starch, millet flour, buckwheat flour, brown rice flour and salt. In a medium bowl, combine the warm water, honey and molasses. Stir in the psyllium husk to form a gel. Immediately whisk the psyllium gel to prevent lumps from forming, then whisk in the cooled oats and levain and add this mixture to the flour blend. Mix the dough well by hand, or with a kitchen mixer fitted with a dough hook running at medium-low speed, until all the ingredients are fully incorporated.

(continued)

Rustic Honey *and* Oat Loaf (continued)

Topping

30 g whole gluten-free oats

Ferment: Form the dough into a ball, then place it in a 4-cup (1-L) proofing bowl. Cover the bowl with its lid and place the bowl in the oven with the light on. Let the dough rest for 30 to 60 minutes, or until the dough begins to rise a little. Place the covered bowl in the fridge overnight for the bulk fermentation.

Shape: The next day, remove the dough from the fridge and leave it at room temperature for about 30 minutes, until it is warm enough to work with. Liberally dust a 7-inch (18-cm) banneton with the white rice flour. Lightly dampen a work surface with water. Transfer the dough to the prepared work surface. Knead the dough with wet hands for 2 to 3 minutes, and then shape it into a ball. Sprinkle a little of the white rice flour on the dough's surface, then repeat the kneading process for about 1 minute. With cupped hands, drag the dough in small circles to shape it into a smooth ball. Pinch, seal and smooth any seams in the dough. Scoop the dough up with a bench scraper and gently place it seam side up in the prepared banneton.

Proof: Place the dough, still in the banneton, inside a reusable plastic bag and let it rest at room temperature—ideally about 72°F (22°C)—for 3 to 5 hours. The proofing time depends on the temperature of your kitchen. If the temperature is a little colder, place the dough in the oven with the light on. In the summer warmth, it can be left on the counter, and it may benefit from less proofing time. When the dough has proofed enough, it will have risen and will feel soft, puffy and spongy on the sides and in the center. Chill the dough in the refrigerator for 30 minutes before baking it to create a little more oven spring.

Score: If you will be baking the bread in a Dutch oven, preheat the oven to 450°F (232°C) with a Dutch oven inside. Meanwhile, cut out some parchment paper for the dough to sit on. Place the parchment paper on top of the dough, which should still be in the banneton. Flip the banneton upside down, so that the parchment paper is underneath to hold the dough, and remove the banneton. Lightly dampen the surface of the dough with wet fingers. Sprinkle some white rice flour on the dough, then evenly spread the flour around the top of the dough with your hands. Slash a square around the top of the dough, then moisten only the center of the square with water and sprinkle the whole oats inside the square area.

Bake: Gently slide the parchment paper with the dough into the Dutch oven. Cover the Dutch oven and bake the bread for 25 minutes to steam it. Reduce the oven's temperature to 400°F (204°C), remove the Dutch oven's lid to allow the loaf to brown and bake the loaf for 30 to 35 minutes, or until the loaf feels firm.

Place the hot sourdough on a wire rack to cool for at least 2 hours before slicing it.

Wrap the bread in a tea towel or beeswax wraps and store it on the counter for 2 to 3 days. If your sourdough begins to dry out too quickly, it is best to slice and freeze the remainder. The sourdough will last in the freezer for up to 3 months.

Dark Sunflower Loaf

Dark, bold and slightly tangy, this loaf is made with gluten-free ingredients to mimic the dark rye breads I remember loving before I was diagnosed with celiac disease. It is loaded with sunflower seeds, and it makes a satiating start to the day. As you prepare the dough, the aromas of coffee and cocoa are amazing, but they do not overpower the taste of the loaf after it is baked. My favorite way to eat this bread is with gluten-free VEGEMITE and avocado, but it is still perfect as a savory sandwich for lunch.

In this recipe, a small amount of quinoa flour has been added to the levain to boost its activity, but you can substitute this with more buckwheat flour if you like. There is also a small amount of sourdough starter discard included to boost the tanginess of the dough.

Makes 1 loaf

Levain

30 g active starter

60 g warm water

20 g buckwheat flour

30 g brown rice flour

10 g quinoa flour

Loaf

40 g raw unsalted sunflower seeds

½ tsp fresh lemon juice, at room temperature

50 g brewed coffee, at room temperature

70 g tapioca starch

50 g buckwheat flour

55 g brown rice flour

55 g sorghum flour

40 g millet flour

30 g teff flour

25 g oat flour

15 g brown sugar

10 g unsweetened cocoa powder

Reactivate your starter the day before you plan on building the levain. A good time to do this is when you get up in the morning, to allow the starter 6 to 8 hours to become bubbly and active. You will need 30 grams for the levain and at least 20 grams for maintaining your original starter/main culture (see page 14 for more information on the feeding ratio).

Build the levain: Using a kitchen scale, weigh 30 grams of active starter in a clean 500-milliliter jar. Add 60 grams of warm water and vigorously whisk the starter and water together. Add 20 grams of buckwheat flour, 30 grams of brown rice flour and 10 grams of quinoa flour. Ferment the levain for 6 to 8 hours, or until it is bubbly and has risen to a peak, before mixing it into the dough.

Mix the dough: In a small bowl, soak the sunflower seeds in the lemon juice and coffee as you prepare the rest of the ingredients. This softens the seeds and creates a better bread texture. In a large bowl, combine the tapioca starch, buckwheat flour, brown rice flour, sorghum flour, millet flour, teff flour, oat flour, brown sugar, cocoa powder and salt. In a medium bowl, combine the warm water, molasses and olive oil. Stir in the psyllium husk and flaxseed to form a gel. Immediately whisk the psyllium gel to prevent lumps from forming, then whisk in the levain and the starter discard. Add this mixture to the flour blend. Stir in the soaked sunflower seeds and caraway seeds (if using) and combine everything well by hand, or with a kitchen mixer fitted with a dough hook running at medium-low speed, until all the ingredients are fully incorporated.

(continued)

Loaf (cont.)

10 g salt

310 g warm water

20 g molasses, at room temperature

10 g olive oil

18 g whole psyllium husk

5 g flaxseed, finely ground

130 g starter discard, at room temperature

½ tsp caraway seeds, crushed (optional)

White rice flour, as needed

Ferment: Form the dough into a ball, then place it in a 4-cup (1-L) proofing bowl. Cover the bowl with its lid and place the bowl in the oven with the light on. Let the dough rest for 30 to 60 minutes, or until the dough begins to rise a little. Place the covered bowl in the fridge overnight for the bulk fermentation.

Shape: The next day, remove the dough from the fridge and leave it at room temperature for about 30 minutes, until it is warm enough to work with. Liberally dust a 7-inch (18-cm) banneton with the white rice flour. Lightly dampen a work surface with water. Transfer the dough to the work surface. Knead the dough with wet hands for 2 to 3 minutes, and then shape it into a ball. Sprinkle a little of the white rice flour on the dough's surface, then repeat the kneading process for about 1 minute. With cupped hands, drag the dough in small circles to shape it into a smooth ball. Pinch, seal and smooth any seams in the dough. Scoop the dough up with a bench scraper and gently place it seam side up in the prepared banneton.

Proof: Place the dough, still in the banneton, inside a reusable plastic bag and let it rest at room temperature—ideally about 72°F (22°C)—for 3 to 5 hours. The proofing time depends on the temperature of your kitchen. If the temperature is a little colder, place the dough in the oven with the light on. In the summer warmth, it can be left on the counter, and it may benefit from less proofing time. When the dough has proofed enough, it will have risen and will feel soft, puffy and spongy on the sides and in the center. Chill the dough for about 30 minutes in the refrigerator before baking it to create a little more oven spring.

Score: If you will be baking the bread in a Dutch oven, preheat the oven to 450°F (232°C) with a Dutch oven inside. Meanwhile, cut out some parchment paper for the dough to sit on. Place the parchment paper on top of the dough, which should still be in the banneton. Flip the banneton upside down, so that the parchment paper is underneath to hold the dough, and remove the banneton. Lightly dampen the surface of the dough with wet fingers. Sprinkle some white rice flour on the dough, then evenly spread the flour around the top of the dough with your hands. Slash very shallow, thin squiggly lines all over the top of the dough to mimic the appearance of rye bread.

Bake: Gently slide the parchment paper with the dough into the Dutch oven. Cover the Dutch oven and bake the loaf for 25 minutes. Reduce the oven's temperature to 400°F (204°F), remove the Dutch oven's lid and bake the bread for 25 to 30 minutes. When the bread is done, it will be brown, have a crispy crust and will sound hollow when it is tapped on the bottom.

Place the hot sourdough on a wire rack to cool for at least 2 hours before slicing it.

Wrap the bread in a tea towel or beeswax wraps and store it on the counter for 2 to 3 days. If your sourdough begins to dry out too quickly, it is best to slice and freeze the remainder. The sourdough will last in the freezer for up to 3 months.

Seeded Sourdough Loaf

The springy softness of this sourdough loaf is packed full of seeds and gluten-free grains that make it very satisfying. After shaping the dough, roll it in a thick layer of seeds to provide texture and a nutty flavor that's so good you simply will not be able to stop at just one slice. This bread is ideal for sandwiches, but it's also delicious toasted or eaten while it's still warm. Normally, I recommend allowing the loaves to cool completely before slicing them, but not this one! A slice from this loaf is amazing warm, but it's equally as good for a sandwich the next day.

Makes 1 loaf

Levain

60 g active starter

120 g warm water

60 g buckwheat flour

60 g brown rice flour

Loaf

60 g milk, cold or straight from the fridge

20 g honey

10 g molasses

80 g sorghum flour

30 g buckwheat flour

60 g oat flour

60 g tapioca starch

10 g teff flour

7 g salt

180 g warm water

14 g whole psyllium husk

6 g flaxseed, finely ground

White rice flour, as needed

Reactivate your starter the day before you plan on building the levain. A good time to do this is when you get up in the morning, to allow the starter 6 to 8 hours to become bubbly and active. You will need 60 grams for the levain and at least 20 grams for maintaining your original starter/main culture (see page 14 for more information on the feeding ratio).

Build the levain: Using a kitchen scale, weigh 60 grams of active starter in a clean 750-milliliter jar. Add 120 grams of warm water and vigorously mix the starter and water together, then add 60 grams of buckwheat flour and 60 grams of brown rice flour. Ferment the levain for 6 to 8 hours, or until it is bubbly and has risen to a peak, before mixing it into the dough.

Mix the dough: In a medium saucepan over medium heat, warm the milk, honey and molasses to about 86°F (30°C). This mixture will take only about 1 minute to warm up. Do not get the liquid too hot (more than 93°F [34°C]) because doing so may kill the natural yeast in the levain. Allow the mixture to cool in the saucepan until it is lukewarm. Meanwhile, in a large bowl, combine the sorghum flour, buckwheat flour, oat flour, tapioca starch, teff flour and salt. Add the warm water to the cooled mixture in the saucepan and stir in the psyllium husk and flaxseed to form a gel. Immediately whisk the psyllium gel to prevent lumps from forming, then whisk in the levain and add this mixture to the flour blend. Mix the dough well by hand, or with a kitchen mixer fitted with a dough hook running at medium-low speed, until all the ingredients are fully incorporated.

Ferment: Form the dough into a ball, then place it in a 4-cup (1-L) proofing bowl. Cover the bowl with its lid and place the bowl in the oven with the light on. Let the dough rest for 30 to 60 minutes, or until the dough begins to rise a little. Place the covered bowl in the fridge overnight for the bulk fermentation.

(continued)

Seeded *Sourdough* Loaf (continued)

Toppings

Toasted, salted and peppered pumpkin seeds and sunflower seeds

Shape: The next day, remove the dough from the fridge and leave it at room temperature for about 30 minutes, until it is warm enough to work with. Liberally dust a 7-inch (18-cm) banneton with the white rice flour, then add a thin layer of pumpkin seeds and sunflower seeds on the bottom to create the bread's topping. Lightly dampen a work surface with water. Transfer the dough to the prepared work surface. Knead the dough with wet hands for 2 to 3 minutes, and then shape it into a ball. Sprinkle a little white rice flour on the dough's surface, then repeat the kneading process for about 1 minute. With cupped hands, drag the dough in small circles to shape it into a smooth ball. Pinch, seal and smooth any seams in the dough. Scoop the dough up with a bench scraper and gently place it seam side up in the prepared banneton.

Proof: Place the dough, still in the banneton, inside a reusable plastic bag and let it rest at room temperature—ideally about 72°F (22°C)—for 3 to 5 hours. The proofing time depends on the temperature of your kitchen. If the temperature is a little colder, place the dough in the oven with the light on. In the summer warmth, it can be left on the counter, and it may benefit from less proofing time. When the dough has proofed enough, it will have risen and will feel soft, puffy and spongy on the sides and in the center. Chill the dough in the refrigerator for 30 minutes before baking it to create a little more oven spring.

Score: If you will be baking the bread in a Dutch oven, preheat the oven to 450°F (232°C) with a Dutch oven inside. Meanwhile, cut out some parchment paper for the dough to sit on. Place the parchment paper on top of the dough, which should still be in the banneton. Flip the banneton upside down, so that the parchment paper is underneath to hold the dough, and remove the banneton. Lightly dampen the surface of the dough with wet fingers. Sprinkle some white rice flour over the dough, then evenly spread the flour around the top of the dough with your hands. Score a pattern on the loaf with a bread lame.

Bake: Gently slide the parchment paper with the dough into the Dutch oven. Cover the Dutch oven and bake the loaf for 25 minutes. Remove the Dutch oven's lid, reduce the oven's temperature to 400°F (204°C) and bake the bread for 25 to 30 minutes, or until the bread is golden brown and feels firm.

Place the hot sourdough on a wire rack to cool for at least 30 minutes before slicing it.

Wrap the bread in a tea towel or beeswax wraps and store it on the counter for 2 to 3 days. If your sourdough begins to dry out too quickly, it is best to slice and freeze the remainder. The sourdough will last in the freezer for up to 3 months.

Golden Tahini Loaf

Golden and buttery tahini is a star in this spectacular sourdough loaf. Here's a bread that caters to not just a gluten intolerance but also to a nut allergy without skimping on flavor. Tahini is made from ground hulled sesame seeds that have been toasted. This gluten-free, homemade version of the classic paste is quick and easy to make. When you add the tahini to the sourdough, the bread turns a gorgeous golden color from the toasted seeds. The aroma of the dough astounds me each time I make this recipe. Tahini has such an exquisite nutty aroma and a flavor comparable to peanut butter, so there is no need to add anything else after baking— although this bread is incredibly good spread with butter, coconut oil or some leftover tahini paste.

Makes 1 loaf

Levain

40 g active starter

80 g warm water

40 g buckwheat flour

40 g brown rice flour

Tahini

70 g raw hulled sesame seeds

45 g olive oil

5 g soy sauce

Loaf

40 g brown rice flour

60 g sorghum flour

70 g tapioca starch

40 g buckwheat flour

30 g quinoa flour

50 g oat flour

7 g salt

280 g warm water

60 g milk, at room temperature

30 g brown sugar

19 g whole psyllium husk

6 g flaxseed, finely ground

20 g melted coconut oil

Reactivate your starter the day before you plan on building the levain. A good time to do this is when you get up in the morning, to allow the starter 6 to 8 hours to become bubbly and active. You will need 40 grams for the levain and at least 20 grams for maintaining your original starter/main culture (see page 14 for more information).

Build the levain: Using a kitchen scale, weigh 40 grams of active starter in a clean 500-milliliter jar. Add 80 grams of warm water and vigorously whisk it with the starter. Add 40 grams of buckwheat flour and 40 grams of brown rice flour. Ferment the levain for 6 to 8 hours, or until it is bubbly and has risen to a peak, before mixing it into the dough.

Make the tahini: In a small skillet over medium-low heat, toast the sesame seeds in the olive oil and soy sauce for 5 to 6 minutes, stirring the sesame seeds continuously, as they will easily burn, until they are golden brown. Let the sesame seeds, olive oil and soy sauce cool completely, then transfer them to a small blender. Blend the sesame seeds, olive oil and sory sauce into a fine paste. You will only need 60 grams of this tahini for the dough; the remainder can be stored in the fridge to be used as a spread on toast.

Mix the dough: In a large bowl, combine the brown rice flour, sorghum flour, tapioca starch, buckwheat flour, quinoa flour, oat flour and salt. In a medium bowl, combine the warm water, milk and brown sugar. Stir in the psyllium husk, ground flaxseed and melted coconut oil to form a gel. Immediately whisk the psyllium gel to prevent lumps from forming, then whisk in the levain and 60 grams of tahini and add this mixture to the flour blend. Mix the dough well by hand, or with a kitchen mixer fitted with a dough hook running at medium-low speed, until all the ingredients are fully incorporated.

Ferment: Form the dough into a ball, then place it in a 4-cup (1-L) proofing bowl. Cover the bowl with its lid and put the bowl in the oven with the light on. Let the dough rest for 30 to 60 minutes, or until the dough begins to rise a little. Place the covered bowl in the fridge overnight for the bulk fermentation.

(continued)

Golden Tahini Loaf (continued)

Loaf (cont.)

White rice flour, as needed

Shape: The next day, remove the dough from the fridge and leave it at room temperature for about 30 minutes, until it is warm enough to work with. Liberally dust a 7-inch (18-cm) banneton with the white rice flour. Lightly dampen a work surface with water. Transfer the dough to the prepared work surface. Knead the dough with wet hands for 2 to 3 minutes, and then shape it into a ball. Sprinkle a little white rice flour on the dough's surface, then repeat the kneading process for about 1 minute. With cupped hands, drag the dough in small circles to shape it into a smooth ball. Pinch, seal and smooth any seams in the dough. Scoop the dough up with a bench scraper and gently place it seam side up in the prepared banneton.

Proof: Place the dough, still in the banneton, inside a reusable plastic bag and let it rest at room temperature—ideally about 72°F (22°C)—for 3 to 5 hours. The proofing time depends on the temperature of your kitchen. If the temperature is a little colder, place the dough in the oven with the light on. In the summer warmth, it can be left on the counter, and it may benefit from less proofing time. When the dough has proofed enough, it will have risen and will feel soft, puffy and spongy on the sides and in the center. Chill the dough in the refrigerator for 30 minutes before baking it to create a little more oven spring.

Score: If you will be baking the bread in a Dutch oven, preheat the oven to 450°F (232°C) with a Dutch oven inside. Meanwhile, cut out some parchment paper for the dough to sit on. Place the parchment paper on top of the dough, which should still be in the banneton. Flip the banneton upside down, so that the parchment paper is underneath to hold the dough, and remove the banneton. Lightly dampen the surface of the dough with wet fingers. Sprinkle some white rice flour on the dough, then evenly spread the flour around the top of the dough with your hands. Score a windmill pattern around the top of the dough.

Bake: Gently slide the paper with the dough into the Dutch oven. Cover the Dutch oven and bake the loaf for 25 minutes. Reduce the oven's temperature to 400°F (204°C), remove the Dutch oven's lid to allow the loaf to brown and bake the loaf for 30 to 35 minutes, or until the loaf feels firm.

Place the hot sourdough on a wire rack to cool for at least 2 hours before slicing it.

Wrap the bread in a tea towel or beeswax wraps and store it on the counter for 2 to 3 days. If your sourdough begins to dry out too quickly, it is best to slice and freeze the remainder. The sourdough will last in the freezer for up to 3 months.

Buckwheat *and* Rosemary Loaf

This aromatic bread utilizes fresh rosemary for optimal flavor. It contains a large amount of buckwheat flour, which gives this satisfying loaf a nice density and a texture that will sustain you throughout the day. Buckwheat makes an amazing gluten-free flour that is a good source of protein, minerals and antioxidants. You will find it extremely hard not to slice into this enticing loaf while it is warm—it smells and tastes so delicious! It is especially good for sandwiches to take with you if you are on the go and worried about finding gluten-free foods in restaurants.

Makes 1 loaf

Levain

40 g active starter

80 g warm water

40 g buckwheat flour

40 g brown rice flour

Loaf

100 g buckwheat flour

70 g tapioca starch

30 g almond flour

30 g quinoa flour

7 g salt

260 g warm water

30 g olive oil

30 g brown sugar

23 g whole psyllium husk

2 g finely chopped fresh rosemary

White rice flour, as needed

Reactivate your starter the day before you plan on building the levain. A good time to do this is when you get up in the morning, to allow the starter 6 to 8 hours to become bubbly and active. You will need 40 grams for the levain and at least 20 grams left over for maintaining your original starter/main culture (see page 14 for more information on the feeding ratio).

Build the levain: Using a kitchen scale, weigh 40 grams of active starter in a clean 500-milliliter jar. Add 80 grams of warm water and vigorously whisk the starter and water together. Add 40 grams of buckwheat flour and 40 grams of brown rice flour. Ferment the levain for 6 to 8 hours, or until it is bubbly and has risen to a peak, before mixing it into the dough.

Mix the dough: In a large bowl, combine the buckwheat flour, tapioca starch, almond flour, quinoa flour and salt. In a medium bowl, combine the warm water, olive oil and brown sugar. Stir in the psyllium husk to form a gel. Immediately whisk the psyllium gel to prevent lumps from forming, then whisk in the levain and add this mixture to the flour blend. Add the rosemary and mix the dough well by hand, or with a kitchen mixer fitted with a dough hook running at medium-low speed, until all the ingredients are fully incorporated.

Ferment: Form the dough into a ball, then place it into a 4-cup (1-L) proofing bowl. Cover the bowl with its lid and place it in the oven with the light on. Let the dough rest for 30 to 60 minutes, or until the dough begins to rise a little. Place the covered bowl in the fridge overnight for the bulk fermentation.

(continued)

Shape: The next day, remove the dough from the fridge and leave it at room temperature for about 30 minutes, until it is warm enough to work with. Liberally dust a 7-inch (18-cm) banneton with the white rice flour. Lightly dampen a work surface with water. Transfer the dough to the prepared surface. Knead the dough with wet hands for 2 to 3 minutes, and then shape it into a ball. Sprinkle a little white rice flour on the dough's surface, then repeat the kneading process for about 1 minute. With cupped hands, drag the dough in small circles to shape it into a smooth ball. Pinch, seal and smooth any seams in the dough. Scoop the dough up with a bench scraper and gently place it seam side up in the prepared banneton.

Proof: Place the dough, still in the banneton, inside a reusable plastic bag and let it rest at room temperature—ideally about 72°F (22°C)—for 3 to 5 hours. The proofing time depends on the temperature of your kitchen. If the temperature is a little colder, place the dough in the oven with the light on. In the summer warmth, it can be left on the counter, and it may benefit from less proofing time. When the dough has proofed enough, it will have risen and will feel soft, puffy and spongy on the sides and in the center. Chill the dough in the refrigerator for 30 minutes before baking it to create a little more oven spring.

Score: If you will be baking the bread in a Dutch oven, preheat the oven to 450°F (232°C) with a Dutch oven inside. Meanwhile, cut out some parchment paper for the dough to sit on. Place the parchment paper on top of the dough, which should still be in the banneton. Flip the banneton upside down, so that the parchment paper is underneath to hold the dough, and remove the banneton. Lightly dampen the surface of the dough with wet fingers. Sprinkle some white rice flour on the dough, then evenly spread the flour around the top of the dough with your hands. Score a pattern on the dough with a bread lame.

Bake: Gently slide the paper with the dough into the Dutch oven. Cover the Dutch oven and bake the loaf for 25 minutes. Reduce the oven's temperature to 400°F (204°C), remove the Dutch oven's lid and bake the loaf for 35 minutes. Reduce the oven's temperature to 350°F (177°C). Remove the loaf from the Dutch oven, place the loaf on the oven's center rack and bake it for 10 minutes, or until the loaf feels firm.

Place the hot sourdough on a wire rack to cool for at least 2 hours before slicing it.

Wrap the bread in a tea towel or beeswax wraps and store it on the counter for 2 to 3 days. If your sourdough begins to dry out too quickly, it is best to slice and freeze the remainder. The sourdough will last in the freezer for up to 3 months.

Fennel *and* Sesame Loaf

Gluten-free bread has never looked or tasted so amazing. This is an appetizing loaf with the subtle aroma of fennel and a light flavor comparable to anise or licorice. Fennel is a sweet-smelling herb native to the Mediterranean region and is often used in pasta sauces, sausages, curries and other dishes. Fennel is also well known as a digestion aid, and I have always been attracted to its smell. If it is not to your liking, it can easily be substituted with cumin seeds, dill seeds or caraway seeds.

A fun option for this bread is to split the dough in half before shaping it and then add some activated charcoal to one piece before combining the two halves back together for a black-and-white variegated loaf, like I've chosen to make!

Makes 1 loaf

Levain

60 g active starter

120 g warm water

60 g buckwheat flour

60 g brown rice flour

Loaf

80 g sorghum flour

30 g buckwheat flour

60 g oat flour

60 g tapioca starch

20 g teff flour

9 g salt

60 g cold milk

20 g molasses, at room temperature

235 g warm water

30 g olive oil, at room temperature

18 g whole psyllium husk

7 g flaxseed, finely ground

1 tsp fennel seeds, crushed

1 tsp raw sesame seeds

5 g activated charcoal (optional)

White rice flour, as needed

Reactivate your starter the day before you plan on building the levain. A good time to do this is when you get up in the morning, to allow the starter 6 to 8 hours to become bubbly and active. You will need 60 grams for the levain and at least 20 grams left over for maintaining your original starter/main culture (see page 14 for more information on the feeding ratio).

Build the levain: Using a kitchen scale, weigh 60 grams of active starter in a clean 750-milliliter jar. Vigorously whisk in 120 grams of warm water, then add 60 grams of buckwheat flour and 60 grams of brown rice flour. Ferment the levain for 6 to 8 hours, or until it is bubbly and has risen to a peak, before mixing it into the dough.

Mix the dough: In a large bowl, combine the sorghum flour, buckwheat flour, oat flour, tapioca starch, teff flour and salt. In a medium pot over medium heat, combine the cold milk and molasses. Warm the mixture to about 86°F (30°C)—you can check the temperature by using a thermometer or by touching the liquid, which should be neither too hot nor too cold. The mixture will take only about 1 minute to warm up. In a medium bowl, combine the warm water and olive oil. Stir in the psyllium husk, flaxseed, fennel seeds and sesame seeds to form a gel. Immediately whisk the psyllium gel to prevent lumps from forming, then whisk in the levain and milk-molasses mixture. Add this mixture to the flour blend. Mix the dough well by hand, or with a kitchen mixer fitted with a dough hook running at medium-low speed, until all the ingredients are fully incorporated.

If you'd like a black-and-white variegated loaf, split the dough in half and add the activated charcoal (if using) to only one-half of the dough. If you are not adding charcoal, then shape the dough into a ball.

(continued)

Fennel *and* Sesame Loaf (continued)

Ferment: Form the dough into a ball, then place it in a 4-cup (1-L) proofing bowl or two separate bowls if using charcoal. Cover the bowl with its lid and place the bowl in the oven with the light on. Let the dough rest for 30 to 60 minutes, or until the dough begins to rise a little. Place the covered bowl in the fridge overnight for the bulk fermentation.

Shape: The next day, remove the dough from the fridge and leave it at room temperature for about 30 minutes, until it is warm enough to work with. Liberally dust a 7-inch (18-cm) banneton with the white rice flour. Lightly dampen a work surface with water. Transfer the dough to the prepared work surface. Knead the dough with wet hands for 2 to 3 minutes, and then shape it into a ball. If using charcoal, knead each ball separately and then spread out each piece of dough into an 8 x 10–inch (20 x 25–cm) rectangle, placing the charcoal dough on top of the lighter dough before shaping it into a single ball. Sprinkle a little white rice flour on the dough's surface, then repeat the kneading process for about 1 minute. With cupped hands, drag the dough in small circles to shape it into a smooth ball. Pinch, seal and smooth any seams in the dough. Scoop the dough up with a bench scraper and gently place it seam side up in the prepared banneton.

Proof: Place the dough, still in the banneton, inside a reusable plastic bag and let it rest at room temperature—ideally about 72°F (22°C)—for 3 to 5 hours. The proofing time depends on the temperature of your kitchen. If the temperature is a little colder, place the dough in the oven with the light on. In the summer warmth, it can be left on the counter, and it may benefit from less proofing time. When the dough has proofed enough, it will have risen and will feel soft, puffy and spongy on the sides and in the center. Chill the dough in the refrigerator for 30 minutes before baking it to create a little more oven spring.

Score: If you will be baking the bread in a Dutch oven, preheat the oven to 450°F (232°C) with a Dutch oven inside. Meanwhile, cut out some parchment paper for the dough to sit on. Place the parchment paper on top of the dough, which should still be in the banneton. Flip the banneton upside down, so that the parchment paper is underneath to hold the dough, and remove the banneton. Lightly dampen the surface of the dough with wet fingers. Sprinkle some white rice flour on the dough, then evenly spread the flour around the top of the dough with your hands. Score a design on top of the dough.

Bake: Gently slide the paper with the dough into the Dutch oven. Cover the Dutch oven with its lid and bake the loaf for 25 minutes to steam the bread. Reduce the oven's temperature to 400°F (204°C), remove the Dutch oven's lid to allow the loaf to brown and bake the bread for 35 minutes, or until the loaf feels firm. The loaf will be light brown in color with crispy edges.

Place the hot sourdough on a wire rack to cool for at least 2 hours before slicing it.

Wrap the bread in a tea towel or beeswax wraps and store it on the counter for 2 to 3 days. If your sourdough begins to dry out too quickly, it is best to slice and freeze the remainder. The sourdough will last in the freezer for up to 3 months.

Sourdough Whey Loaf

Gut-healthy yogurt and sourdough, both fermented foods packed with good bacteria, make this loaf of sourdough whey too good! Using yogurt is an easy way to soften the crumb, and this gluten-free sourdough bread has an incredibly soft and airy feel—the beautifully light texture and crumb is reminiscent of old-fashioned white bread. There is a slightly more pronounced tanginess from the addition of the yogurt, but the flavor is still subtle and light. Everything pairs with this versatile bread.

This recipe requires two levain feedings.

Makes 1 loaf

Morning Levain Feeding

30 g active starter

35 g warm water

15 g brown rice flour

15 g buckwheat flour

Afternoon Levain Feeding

95 g levain from the morning feeding

55 g warm water

25 g brown rice flour

25 g buckwheat flour

Yogurt

250 g plain, unsweetened full-fat Greek yogurt

Reactivate your starter the day before you plan on building the levain. A good time to do this is right before bed, to allow the starter 6 to 8 hours to become bubbly and active. You will need 30 grams for the levain and at least 20 grams left over for maintaining your original starter/main culture (see page 14 for more information on the feeding ratio).

Build the levain: This is done in two stages. For the morning levain feeding, use a kitchen scale to weigh 30 grams of active starter in a clean 500-milliliter jar. Add 35 grams of warm water, 15 grams of brown rice flour and 15 grams of buckwheat flour. Mix everything together well.

For the afternoon levain feeding, put the 95 grams of levain from the morning feeding in a clean 500-milliliter jar. Add 55 grams of warm water, 25 grams of brown rice flour and 25 grams of buckwheat flour. Ferment the levain for 6 to 8 hours, or until it is bubbly and has risen to a peak, before mixing it into the dough.

Strain the yogurt: Strain the Greek yogurt after you feed the levain the second time. Place a medium bowl covered with a sieve or piece of cheesecloth on a kitchen scale. Spoon the Greek yogurt into the sieve, then cover the top of the sieve and leave the yogurt to drain while the levain rises, which will take 3 to 5 hours. You may need to strain the yogurt in the fridge if your kitchen's temperature is above 65°F (18°C).

(continued)

Loaf

100 g strained plain, unsweetened full-fat Greek yogurt

50 g strained whey (the liquid from the full-fat Greek yogurt)

90 g brown rice flour

40 g sweet white rice flour

75 g tapioca starch

50 g oat flour

25 g quinoa flour

6 g salt

180 g warm water

20 g olive oil

20 g pure maple syrup

23 g whole psyllium husk

5 g flaxseed, finely ground

White rice flour, as needed

Mix the dough: Weigh the strained Greek yogurt and the liquid whey each in a medium bowl. Because of variations in yogurt brands, you may have less than 50 grams of whey to use. If you are a little short on whey, you can add water to make the correct amount. If there is a little more yogurt than the recipe calls for, then just eat it for a quick snack. In a large bowl, combine the brown rice flour, sweet white rice flour, tapioca starch, oat flour, quinoa flour and salt. To the bowl of whey, add the warm water, olive oil and maple syrup. Stir in the psyllium husk and flaxseed to form a gel. Immediately whisk the psyllium gel to prevent lumps from forming, then whisk in the levain and the strained yogurt. Add this mixture to the flour blend. Mix the dough well by hand, or with a kitchen mixer fitted with a dough hook running at medium-low speed, until all the ingredients are fully incorporated.

Ferment: Form the dough into a ball, then place it in a 4-cup (1-L) proofing bowl. Cover the bowl with its lid and place it in the oven with the light on. Let the dough rest for 30 to 60 minutes, or until the dough begins to rise a little. Place the covered bowl in the fridge overnight for the bulk fermentation.

Shape: The next day, remove the dough from the fridge and leave it at room temperature for about 30 minutes, until it is warm enough to work with. Liberally dust a 7-inch (18-cm) banneton with the white rice flour. Lightly dampen a work surface with water. Transfer the dough to the prepared work surface. Knead the dough with wet hands for 2 to 3 minutes, and then shape it into a ball. Sprinkle a little white rice flour on the dough's surface, then repeat the kneading process for about 1 minute. With cupped hands, drag the dough in small circles to shape it into a smooth ball. Pinch, seal and smooth any seams in the dough. Scoop the dough up with a bench scraper and gently place it seam side up in the prepared banneton.

Proof: Place the dough, still in the banneton, inside a reusable plastic bag and let it rest at room temperature—ideally about 72°F (22°C)—for 3 to 5 hours. The proofing time depends on the temperature of your kitchen. If the temperature is a little colder, place the dough in the oven with the light on. In the summer warmth, it can be left on the counter, and it may benefit from less proofing time. When the dough has proofed enough, it will have risen and will feel soft, puffy and spongy on the sides and in the center. Chill the dough in the refrigerator for 30 minutes before baking it to create a little more oven spring.

Score: If you will be baking the bread in a Dutch oven, preheat the oven to 450°F (232°C) with a Dutch oven inside. Meanwhile, cut out some parchment paper for the dough to sit on. Place the parchment paper on top of the dough, which should still be in the banneton. Flip the banneton upside down, so that the parchment paper is underneath to hold the dough, and remove the banneton. Lightly dampen the dough with wet fingers. Sprinkle some white rice flour on the dough, then evenly spread the flour around the top of the dough with your hands. Score a design on the top of the dough.

Bake: Gently slide the paper with the dough into the Dutch oven. Cover the Dutch oven with its lid and bake the loaf for 25 minutes to steam the bread. Reduce the oven's temperature to 400°F (204°C), remove the Dutch oven's lid to allow the loaf to brown and bake the loaf for 35 minutes, or until the loaf feels firm. The loaf will be light brown in color with crispy edges.

Place the hot sourdough on a wire rack to cool for at least 2 hours before slicing it.

Wrap the bread in a tea towel or beeswax wraps and store it on the counter for 2 to 3 days. If your sourdough begins to dry out too quickly, it is best to slice and freeze the remainder. The sourdough will last in the freezer for up to 3 months.

rustic, full-flavored breads

Once you are more comfortable with baking a loaf of sourdough, it is time to get more creative! There are so many possibilities when adding flavors to sourdough—mixing in herbs, spices, fruit or vegetables transforms a plain loaf of gluten-free sourdough into a miraculously flavored bread that will have everyone reaching for more. There are different methods to incorporate mix-ins to your dough, but I prefer to add my mix-ins directly after combining all the ingredients to allow the flavors to seep into the bread while it ferments. You can choose to incorporate the mix-ins after the fermentation to get a slightly better bread crumb, but the flavors of the mix-ins won't be quite as strong.

When using dried fruit, it is better to soak the fruit for 20 to 30 minutes in warm water or orange juice because they become juicier and plumper as they absorb the moisture—this way, they also do not take moisture from the dough. This soaking technique is used for the Cranberry and Hazelnut Bread (page 63), which is one of my absolute favorite recipes in this book! When using nuts, lightly toasting them in a skillet for extra nutty flavor yields a tastier loaf. Try this technique in my Autumn Walnut and Apple Bread (page 54).

Some of the recipes in this chapter incorporate two levain feedings to boost the activity of the dough.

Autumn Walnut *and* Apple Bread

Fall flavors are packed into this delectable bread! The texture that the apple gives creates a dense but tasty gluten-free bread. I have made this recipe with both Gala and Granny Smith apples, and both are equally good. The addition of apple juice means your bread is infused with apple flavor that merges with the oils and textures of the walnuts. Warm a slice in the toaster and slather on some butter for a tasty snack before you run out the door.

Makes 1 loaf

Levain

40 g active starter

80 g warm water

40 g buckwheat flour

40 g brown rice flour

Loaf

70 g sorghum flour

60 g tapioca starch

60 g buckwheat flour

60 g brown rice flour

30 g millet flour

15 g brown sugar

3 g ground cinnamon

8 g salt

250 g apple juice

100 g warm water

15 g olive oil

25 g pure maple syrup

23 g whole psyllium husk

80 g grated unpeeled Gala or Granny Smith apple

80 g toasted unsalted walnuts

White rice flour, as needed

Reactivate your starter the day before you plan on building the levain. A good time to do this is when you get up in the morning, to allow the starter 6 to 8 hours to become bubbly and active. You will need 40 grams for the levain and at least 20 grams left over for maintaining your original starter/main culture (see page 14 for more information on the feeding ratio).

Build the levain: Using a kitchen scale, weigh 40 grams of active starter in a clean 500-milliliter jar. Vigorously whisk in 80 grams of warm water, then add the 40 grams of buckwheat flour and 40 grams of brown rice flour. Ferment the levain for 6 to 8 hours, or until it is bubbly and has risen to a peak, before mixing it into the dough.

Mix the dough: In a large bowl, combine the sorghum flour, tapioca starch, buckwheat flour, brown rice flour, millet flour, brown sugar, cinnamon and salt. In a medium bowl, combine the apple juice, warm water, olive oil and maple syrup. Stir in the psyllium husk to form a gel. Immediately whisk the psyllium gel to prevent lumps from forming, then whisk in the levain, apple and walnuts. Add this mixture to the flour blend. Mix the dough well by hand, or with a kitchen mixer fitted with a dough hook running at medium-low speed, until all the ingredients are fully incorporated.

Ferment: Form the dough into a ball, then place it in a 4-cup (1-L) proofing bowl. Cover the bowl with its lid and place it in the oven with the light on. Let the dough rest for 30 to 60 minutes, or until the dough begins to rise a little. Place the covered bowl in the fridge overnight for the bulk fermentation.

(continued)

Shape: The next day, remove the dough from the fridge and leave it at room temperature for about 30 minutes, until it is warm enough to work with. Liberally dust a 7-inch (18-cm) banneton with the white rice flour. Lightly dampen a work surface with water. Transfer the dough to the prepared work surface. Knead the dough with wet hands for 2 to 3 minutes, and then shape it into a ball. Sprinkle a little white rice flour on the dough's surface, then repeat the kneading process for about 1 minute. With cupped hands, drag the dough in small circles to shape it into a smooth ball. Pinch, seal and smooth any seams in the dough. Scoop the dough up with a bench scraper and gently place it seam side up in the prepared banneton.

Proof: Place the dough, still in the banneton, inside a reusable plastic bag and let it rest at room temperature—ideally about 72°F (22°C)—for 3 to 5 hours. The proofing time depends on the temperature of your kitchen. If the temperature is a little colder, place the dough in the oven with the light on. In the summer warmth, it can be left on the counter, and it may benefit from less proofing time. When the dough has proofed enough, it will have risen and will feel soft, puffy and spongy on the sides and in the center. Chill the dough in the refrigerator for 30 minutes before baking it to create a little more oven spring.

Score: If you will be baking the bread in a Dutch oven, preheat the oven to 450°F (232°C) with a Dutch oven inside. Meanwhile, cut out some parchment paper for the dough to sit on. Place the parchment paper on top of the dough, which should still be in the banneton. Flip the banneton upside down, so that the parchment paper is underneath to hold the dough, and remove the banneton. Lightly dampen the surface of the dough with wet fingers. Sprinkle some white rice flour on the dough, then evenly spread the flour around the top of the dough with your hands. Score a shallow leaf design on the left side of the dough and score one long, slightly deeper cut along the right side.

Bake: Gently slide the paper with the dough into the Dutch oven. Cover the Dutch oven with its lid and bake the loaf for 25 minutes. Remove the Dutch oven's lid, reduce the oven's temperature to 400°F (204°C) and bake the loaf for 35 minutes. Reduce the oven's temperature to 350°F (177°C) and remove the loaf from the Dutch oven. Place the loaf on the oven's center rack and bake it for 10 minutes, or until it feels firm.

Place the hot sourdough on a wire rack to cool for at least 2 hours before slicing it.

Wrap the bread in a tea towel or beeswax wraps and store it on the counter for 2 to 3 days. If your sourdough begins to dry out too quickly, it is best to slice and freeze the remainder. The sourdough will last in the freezer for up to 3 months.

Beetroot *and* Black Pepper Bread

This loaf has a stunning color and a subtle sweetness from the beets paired with a little heat from the black pepper. It may sound unusual, but the flavor and texture of the bread is remarkable. Cooking the beets the day before baking the loaf helps with the preparation time and gives the beets time to cool. The color of this dough creates a great canvas for your creativity. I love the fact that this gluten-free sourdough version can be made just like regular sourdough. And if you're looking for something to do with the remaining beet water, use it to make borscht!

This recipe requires two levain feedings.

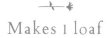

Makes 1 loaf

Morning Levain Feeding

30 g active starter

35 g warm water

15 g brown rice flour

15 g buckwheat flour

Afternoon Levain Feeding

95 g levain from the morning feeding

55 g warm water

25 g brown rice flour

25 g buckwheat flour

Reactivate your starter the day before you plan on building the levain. A good time to do this is right before bed, to allow the starter 6 to 8 hours to become bubbly and active. You will need 30 grams for the levain and at least 20 grams left over for maintaining your original starter/main culture (see page 14 for more information on the feeding ratio).

Build the levain: This is done in two stages. For the morning levain feeding, use a kitchen scale to weigh 30 grams of active starter in a clean 500-milliliter jar. Vigorously mix in 35 grams of warm water, then mix in 15 grams of brown rice flour and 15 grams of buckwheat flour.

For the afternoon levain feeding, keep the 95 grams of levain from the morning feeding in its jar and add 55 grams of warm water, 25 grams of brown rice flour and 25 grams of buckwheat flour. Ferment the levain for 6 to 8 hours, or until it is bubbly and has risen to a peak, before mixing it into the dough.

Mix the dough: In a small blender or food processor, blend the beet with 100 grams of the beet cooking water until a puree forms. In a large bowl, combine the sorghum flour, tapioca starch, buckwheat flour, oat flour, teff flour and salt. In a medium bowl, combine the beet puree, the remaining 150 grams of beet cooking water, maple syrup and olive oil. Stir in the psyllium husk and flaxseed to form a gel. Immediately whisk the psyllium gel to prevent lumps from forming, then whisk in the levain and black pepper. Add this mixture to the flour blend. Mix the dough well by hand, or with a kitchen mixer fitted with a dough hook running at medium-low speed, until all the ingredients are fully incorporated.

(continued)

Beetroot *and* Black Pepper Bread (continued)

Loaf

130 g cooked beet (1 large beet)

250 g beet cooking water, divided

90 g sorghum flour

70 g tapioca starch

30 g buckwheat flour

60 g oat flour

20 g teff flour

9 g salt

30 g pure maple syrup

15 g olive oil

21 g psyllium husk

5 g flaxseed, finely ground

½ tsp black pepper

White rice flour, as needed

Ferment: Form the dough into a ball, then place it in a 4-cup (1-L) proofing bowl. Cover the bowl with its lid and place the bowl in the oven with the light on. Let the dough rest for 30 to 60 minutes, or until the dough begins to rise a little. Place the covered bowl in the fridge overnight for the bulk fermentation.

Shape: The next day, remove the dough from the fridge and leave it at room temperature for about 30 minutes, until it is warm enough to work with. Liberally dust a 7-inch (18-cm) banneton with the white rice flour. Lightly dampen a work surface with water. Transfer the dough to the prepared work surface. Knead the dough with wet hands for 2 to 3 minutes, and then shape it into a ball. Sprinkle a little white rice flour on the dough's surface, then repeat the kneading process for about 1 minute. With cupped hands, drag the dough in small circles to shape it into a smooth ball. Pinch, seal and smooth any seams in the dough. Scoop the dough up with a bench scraper and gently place it seam side up in the prepared banneton.

Proof: Place the dough, still in the banneton, inside a reusable plastic bag and let it rest at room temperature—ideally about 72°F (22°C)—for 3 to 5 hours. The proofing time depends on the temperature of your kitchen. If the temperature is a little colder, place the dough in the oven with the light on. In the summer warmth, it can be left on the counter, and it may benefit from less proofing time. When the dough has proofed enough, it will have risen and will feel soft, puffy and spongy on the sides and in the center. Chill the dough in the refrigerator for 30 minutes before baking it to create a little more oven spring.

Score: If you will be baking the bread in a Dutch oven, preheat the oven to 450°F (232°C) with a Dutch oven inside. Meanwhile, cut out some parchment paper for the dough to sit on. Place the parchment paper on top of the dough, which should still be in the banneton. Flip the banneton upside down, so that the parchment paper is underneath to hold the dough, and remove the banneton. Lightly dampen the surface of the dough with wet fingers. Sprinkle some white rice flour on the dough, then evenly spread the flour around the top of the dough with your hands. Score a heart shape on the dough.

Bake: Gently slide the paper with the dough into the Dutch oven. Cover the Dutch oven with its lid and bake the loaf for 25 minutes. Remove the Dutch oven's lid, reduce the oven's temperature to 400°F (204°C) and bake the loaf for 35 minutes. Reduce the oven's temperature to 350°F (177°C) and remove the loaf from the Dutch oven. Place the loaf on the oven's center rack and bake it for 10 minutes, or until the loaf feels firm.

Place the hot sourdough on a wire rack to cool for at least 2 hours before slicing it.

Wrap the bread in a tea towel or beeswax wraps and store it on the counter for 2 to 3 days. If your sourdough begins to dry out too quickly, it is best to slice and freeze the remainder. The sourdough will last in the freezer for up to 3 months.

Cheese *and* Beer Bread

Combining bread, cheese and beer is an age-old tradition. You must bake this bread, which combines gluten-free dark stout (or your favorite gluten-free beer) with tasty cheese. This bread never lasts long in our house due to the fact that it is so incredibly tasty. It will be gone before two days have passed, so there is no need to worry about how long it will keep. You can finely dice the cheese or grate it, but I personally prefer using grated cheese, which disperses more evenly throughout the bread. If the cheese chunks are too large, they will weigh down the bread and the loaf will not rise as well.

This recipe requires two levain feedings.

Makes 1 loaf

Morning Levain Feeding

20 g active starter

40 g warm water

20 g brown rice flour

20 g buckwheat flour

Afternoon Levain Feeding

100 g levain from the morning feeding

60 g warm water

25 g brown rice flour

25 g buckwheat flour

Reactivate your starter the day before you plan on building the levain. A good time to do this is right before bed, to allow the starter 6 to 8 hours to become bubbly and active. You will need 20 grams for the levain with at least 20 grams left over for maintaining your original starter/main culture (see page 14 for more information on the feeding ratio).

Build the levain: This is done in two stages. For the morning levain feeding, use a kitchen scale to weigh 20 grams of active starter in a clean 750-milliliter jar. Vigorously mix in 40 grams of warm water, 20 grams of brown rice flour and 20 grams of buckwheat flour.

For the afternoon levain feeding, combine the 100 grams of levain from the morning feeding, 60 grams of warm water, 25 grams of brown rice flour and 25 grams of buckwheat flour in the same jar from the morning feeding. Ferment the levain for 6 to 8 hours, or until it is bubbly and has risen to a peak, before mixing it into the dough.

Mix the dough: In a large bowl, combine the buckwheat flour, oat flour, tapioca starch, sorghum flour, millet flour, brown rice flour, teff flour and salt. In a medium bowl, combine the warm water, beer and brown sugar. Stir in the psyllium husk and flaxseed to form a gel. Immediately whisk the psyllium gel to prevent lumps from forming. Whisk in the levain and the Cheddar cheese, then add this mixture to the flour blend. Mix the dough well by hand, or with a kitchen mixer fitted with a dough hook running at medium-low speed, until all the ingredients are fully incorporated.

(continued)

Cheese *and* Beer Bread (continued)

Loaf

35 g buckwheat flour

40 g oat flour

75 g tapioca starch

70 g sorghum flour

40 g millet flour

60 g brown rice flour

20 g teff flour

8 g salt

220 g warm water

200 g gluten-free dark beer or gluten-free beer of choice, at room temperature

20 g brown sugar

23 g whole psyllium husk

5 g flaxseed, finely ground

100 g grated Cheddar or Gouda cheese

White rice flour, as needed

Ferment: Form the dough into a ball, then place it in a 4-cup (1-L) proofing bowl. Cover the bowl with its lid and place it in the oven with the light on. Let the dough rest for 30 to 60 minutes, or until the dough begins to rise a little. Place the covered bowl in the fridge overnight for the bulk fermentation.

Shape: The next day, remove the dough from the fridge and leave it at room temperature for about 30 minutes, until it is warm enough to work with. Liberally dust a 7-inch (18-cm) banneton with the white rice flour. Lightly dampen a work surface with water. Transfer the dough to the prepared work surface. Knead the dough with wet hands for 2 to 3 minutes, and then shape it into a ball. Sprinkle a little white rice flour on the dough's surface, then repeat the kneading process for about 1 minute. With cupped hands, drag the dough in small circles to shape it into a smooth ball. Pinch, seal and smooth any seams in the dough. Scoop the dough up with a bench scraper and gently place it seam side up in the prepared banneton.

Proof: Place the dough, still in the banneton, inside a reusable plastic bag and let it rest at room temperature—ideally about 72°F (22°C)—for 3 to 5 hours. The proofing time depends on the temperature of your kitchen. If the temperature is a little colder, place the dough in the oven with the light on. In the summer warmth, it can be left on the counter, and it may benefit from less proofing time. When the dough has proofed enough, it will have risen and will feel soft, puffy and spongy on the sides and in the center. Chill the dough in the refrigerator for 30 minutes before baking it to create a little more oven spring.

Score: If you will be baking the bread in a Dutch oven, preheat the oven to 450°F (232°C) with a Dutch oven inside. Meanwhile, cut out some parchment paper for the dough to sit on. Place the parchment paper on top of the dough, which should still be in the banneton. Flip the banneton upside down, so that the parchment paper is underneath to hold the dough, and remove the banneton. Lightly dampen the dough's surface with wet fingers. Sprinkle some white rice flour on the dough and smooth out the flour with your hands. With a bread lame or razor blade, score a design in the dough.

Bake: Gently slide the paper with the dough into the Dutch oven. Cover the Dutch oven with its lid and bake the loaf for 20 minutes. Remove the Dutch oven's lid, reduce the oven's temperature to 400°F (204°C) and bake the loaf for 25 to 30 minutes. Reduce the oven's temperature to 350°F (177°C) and bake the bread, still in the Dutch oven, for 10 minutes, or until the loaf feels firm.

Place the hot sourdough on a wire rack to cool for at least 2 hours before slicing it.

Wrap the bread in a tea towel or beeswax wraps and store it on the counter for 3 or 4 days, but keep in mind that this bread is best eaten within 2 days. If your sourdough begins to dry out too quickly, it is best to slice and freeze the remainder. The sourdough will last in the freezer for up to 3 months.

Cranberry *and* Hazelnut Bread

The tartness of cranberries paired with the subtle sweetness of orange and toasted hazelnuts make this an amazing snacking loaf, great for that afternoon energy boost with a cup of tea or coffee. These ingredients combine to give you an unforgettable flavor and texture. A slice of this bread is comparable to a raisin and cinnamon bread but with a more intense flavor and added texture from the nuts. This is a very moreish bread.

When you purchase cranberries, be sure to read the ingredients list on the package to make sure they are not contaminated with gluten.

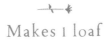

Makes 1 loaf

Levain

60 g active starter

120 g warm water

60 g buckwheat flour

60 g brown rice flour

Loaf

80 g dried cranberries

100 g fresh orange juice, at room temperature

50 g sorghum flour

40 g buckwheat flour

60 g oat flour

65 g tapioca starch

50 g white rice flour, plus more as needed

40 g hazelnuts, roughly chopped

8 g salt

200 g warm water

10 g molasses

20 g honey

18 g whole psyllium husk

5 g flaxseed, finely ground

Reactivate your starter the day before you plan on building the levain. A good time to do this is when you get up in the morning, to allow the starter 6 to 8 hours to become bubbly and active. You will need 60 grams for the levain and at least 20 grams left over for maintaining your original starter/main culture (see page 14 for more information on the feeding ratio).

Build the levain: Using a kitchen scale, weigh 60 grams of active starter in a clean 500-milliliter jar. Add 120 grams of warm water and vigorously whisk the starter and water together. Add 60 grams of buckwheat flour and 60 grams of brown rice flour. Ferment the levain for 6 to 8 hours, or until it is bubbly and has risen to a peak, before mixing it into the dough.

Mix the dough: In a small bowl, soak the cranberries in the orange juice for up to 2 hours or overnight in the fridge to plump them up. In a large bowl, combine the sorghum flour, buckwheat flour, oat flour, tapioca starch, white rice flour, hazelnuts and salt. In a medium bowl, combine the warm water, molasses and honey. Stir in the psyllium husk and flaxseed to form a gel. Immediately whisk the psyllium gel to prevent lumps from forming, then whisk in the levain and cranberries (no need to drain the cranberries, as they should absorb most of the juice). Add this mixture to the flour blend. Mix the dough well by hand, or with a kitchen mixer fitted with a dough hook running at medium-low speed, until all the ingredients are fully incorporated.

Ferment: Form the dough into a ball, then place it in a 4-cup (1-L) proofing bowl. Cover the bowl with its lid and place it in the oven with the light on. Let the dough rest for 30 to 60 minutes, or until the dough begins to rise a little. Place the covered bowl in the fridge overnight for the bulk fermentation.

(continued)

Cranberry *and* Hazelnut Bread (continued)

Shape: The next day, remove the dough from the fridge and leave it at room temperature for about 30 minutes, until it is warm enough to work with. Liberally dust a 7-inch (18-cm) banneton with the additional white rice flour. Lightly dampen a work surface with water. Transfer the dough to the prepared work surface. Knead the dough with wet hands for 2 to 3 minutes, and then shape it into a ball. Sprinkle a little white rice flour on the dough's surface, then repeat the kneading process for about 1 minute. With cupped hands, drag the dough in small circles to shape it into a smooth ball. Poke any exposed cranberries back inside the dough and knead it a little more to smooth its surface. Shape the dough into a ball and gently place the dough seam side up in the prepared banneton.

Proof: Place the dough, still in the banneton, inside a reusable plastic bag and let it rest at room temperature—ideally about 72°F (22°C)—for 3 to 5 hours. The proofing time depends on the temperature of your kitchen. If the temperature is a little colder, place the dough in the oven with the light on. In the summer warmth, it can be left on the counter, and it may benefit from less proofing time. When the dough has proofed enough, it will have risen and will feel soft, puffy and spongy on the sides and in the center. Chill the dough in the refrigerator for 30 minutes before baking it to create a little more oven spring.

Score: If you will be baking the bread in a Dutch oven, preheat the oven to 450°F (232°C) with a Dutch oven inside. Meanwhile, cut out some parchment paper for the dough to sit on. Place the parchment paper on top of the dough, which should still be in the banneton. Flip the banneton upside down, so that the parchment paper is underneath to hold the dough, and remove the banneton. Lightly dampen the surface of the dough with wet fingers. Sprinkle some white rice flour on the dough and smooth out the flour with your hands. With a bread lame or razor blade, score a ½-inch (1.3-cm)-deep cross lined up through the center of the bread.

Bake: Gently place the parchment paper and the dough into the Dutch oven. Cover the Dutch oven with its lid and bake the loaf for 25 minutes. Reduce the oven's temperature to 400°F (204°C), remove the Dutch oven's lid and bake the bread for 25 to 30 minutes. When the bread is done, it will be lightly browned, have a crisp crust and sound hollow when tapped on the bottom.

Place the hot sourdough on a wire rack to cool for at least 2 hours before slicing it.

Wrap the bread in a tea towel or beeswax wraps and store it on the counter for 2 to 3 days. If your sourdough begins to dry out too quickly, it is best to slice it and freeze the remainder. The sourdough will last in the freezer for up to 3 months.

Roasted Garlic *and* Olive Bread

Savory olives soaked in salty, oily brine and then mixed with roasted sweet garlic: These two ingredients form an awesome partnership, and they add a wonderful complexity and depth of flavor to this rustic loaf of gluten-free sourdough. This bread is another of my favorites and is a great addition to any meal. It also makes the best grilled cheese sandwiches, but if you're not in the mood for cooking, it is also spectacular fresh with a large slice of cheese on top.

This recipe requires two levain feedings.

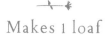

Makes 1 loaf

Morning Levain Feeding

30 g active starter

30 g warm water

15 g buckwheat flour

15 g brown rice flour

Afternoon Levain Feeding

70 g levain (do not use all the morning levain here)

85 g warm water

45 g buckwheat flour

45 g brown rice flour

Loaf

40 g buckwheat flour

70 g brown rice flour

50 g sorghum flour

50 g tapioca starch

35 g millet flour

9 g salt

Reactivate your starter the day before you plan on building the levain. A good time to do this is right before bed, to allow the starter 6 to 8 hours to become bubbly and active. You will need 30 grams for the levain and at least 20 grams left over for maintaining your original starter/main culture (see page 14 for more information on the feeding ratio).

Build the levain: For the morning levain feeding, use a kitchen scale to weigh 30 grams of active starter in a clean 500-milliliter jar. Add 30 grams of warm water and vigorously whisk the ingredients together. Add 15 grams of buckwheat flour and 15 grams of brown rice flour.

For the afternoon levain feeding, add 70 grams of the morning levain to a clean 750-milliliter jar. Add 85 grams of warm water, 45 grams of buckwheat flour and 45 grams of brown rice flour. Vigorously mix the flour, water and starter until they are well combined. Ferment the levain for 6 to 8 hours, or until it is bubbly and has risen to a peak, before mixing it into the dough.

Mix the dough: In a large bowl, combine the buckwheat flour, brown rice flour, sorghum flour, tapioca starch, millet flour and salt. In a small bowl, combine the warm water, olive oil, honey and molasses. Stir in the psyllium husk to form a gel. Immediately whisk the psyllium gel to prevent lumps from forming, then whisk in the levain, black olives and roasted garlic. Add this mixture to the flour blend. Mix the dough well by hand, or with a kitchen mixer fitted with a dough hook running at medium-low speed, until all the ingredients are fully incorporated.

Ferment: Form the dough into a ball, then place it in a 4-cup (1-L) proofing bowl. Cover the bowl with its lid and place it in the oven with the light on. Let the dough rest for 30 to 60 minutes, or until the dough begins to rise a little. Place the covered bowl in the fridge overnight for the bulk fermentation.

(continued)

Roasted Garlic *and* Olive Bread (continued)

Loaf (cont.)

305 g warm water

15 g olive oil

20 g honey

9 g molasses

23 g whole psyllium husk

70 g diced black olives

15 g bulb roasted garlic

White rice flour, as needed

Shape: The next day, remove the dough from the fridge and leave it at room temperature for about 30 minutes, until it is warm enough to work with. Liberally dust a 7-inch (18-cm) banneton with the white rice flour. Lightly dampen a work surface with water. Transfer the dough to the prepared work surface. Knead the dough with wet hands for 2 to 3 minutes, and then shape it into a ball. Sprinkle a little white rice flour on the dough's surface, then repeat the kneading process for about 1 minute. With cupped hands, drag the dough in small circles to shape it into a smooth ball. Pinch, seal and smooth any seams in the dough. Scoop the dough up with a bench scraper and gently place it seam side up in the prepared banneton.

Proof: Place the dough, still in the banneton, inside a reusable plastic bag and let it rest at room temperature—ideally about 72°F (22°C)—for 3 to 5 hours. The proofing time depends on the temperature of your kitchen. If the temperature is a little colder, place the dough in the oven with the light on. In the summer warmth, it can be left on the counter, and it may benefit from less proofing time. When the dough has proofed enough, it will have risen and will feel soft, puffy and spongy on the sides and in the center. Chill the dough in the refrigerator for 30 minutes before baking it to create a little more oven spring.

Score: If you will be baking the bread in a Dutch oven, preheat the oven to 450°F (232°C) with a Dutch oven inside. Meanwhile, cut out some parchment paper for the dough to sit on. Place the parchment paper on top of the dough, which should still be in the banneton. Flip the banneton upside down, so that the parchment paper is underneath to hold the dough, and remove the banneton. Lightly dampen the surface of the dough with wet fingers. Sprinkle some white rice flour on the dough, then evenly spread the flour around the top of the dough with your hands. Score a design on the dough's surface.

Bake: Gently slide the paper with the dough into the Dutch oven. Cover the Dutch oven with its lid and bake the loaf for 25 minutes to steam the bread. Reduce the oven's temperature to 400°F (204°C), remove the Dutch oven's lid to allow the loaf to brown and bake the bread for 30 to 35 minutes, or until the loaf feels firm.

Place the hot sourdough on a wire rack to cool for at least 2 hours before slicing it.

Wrap the bread in a tea towel or beeswax wraps and store it on the counter for 2 to 3 days. If your sourdough begins to dry out too quickly, it is best to slice and freeze the remainder. The sourdough will last in the freezer for up to 3 months.

Pumpkin-Chai Bread

Adding pumpkin puree to this gluten-free sourdough bread gives the dough a silky-smooth texture, but the flavor from the pumpkin is mild. The longer you steep the chai tea, the more prominent the flavor of the chai will be. This bread is amazing served with a bowl of chili or used for a tasty sandwich. This is a seasonal bread but one that you will want to make all year round.

This recipe requires two levain feedings.

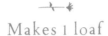

Makes 1 loaf

Morning Levain Feeding

26 g active starter

52 g warm water

26 g buckwheat flour

26 g brown rice flour

Afternoon Levain Feeding

130 g levain from the morning feeding

70 g warm water

25 g sweet white rice flour

25 g brown rice flour

Loaf

65 g sweet white rice flour

70 g tapioca starch

50 g oat flour

40 g millet flour

65 g sorghum flour

9 g salt

1 large egg, at room temperature

150 g warm water

80 g warm steeped chai tea

30 g honey

Reactivate your starter the day before you plan on building the levain. A good time to do this is right before bed, to allow the starter 6 to 8 hours to become bubbly and active. You will need 26 grams for the levain and at least 20 grams left over for maintaining your original starter/main culture (see page 14 for more information on the feeding ratio).

Build the levain: For the morning levain feeding, use a kitchen scale to weigh 26 grams of active starter in a clean 750-milliliter jar. Add 52 grams of warm water and vigorously whisk the starter and water together. Add 26 grams of buckwheat flour and 26 grams of brown rice flour.

For the afternoon levain feeding, you should have 130 grams of levain from the morning's feeding. Add 70 grams of warm water and vigorously mix it with the levain. Add 25 grams of sweet white rice flour and 25 grams of brown rice flour. Ferment the levain for 6 to 8 hours, or until it is bubbly and has risen to a peak, before mixing it into the dough.

Mix the dough: In a large bowl, combine the sweet white rice flour, tapioca starch, oat flour, millet, sorghum flour and salt. In a medium bowl, beat together the egg, warm water, warm chai tea, honey and olive oil, then whisk in the levain. Stir the psyllium husk into the levain mixture and immediately whisk everything together to prevent lumps from forming. Add the pumpkin puree and mix everything together well. Add the chai tea mixture to the flour blend. Mix the dough well by hand, or with a kitchen mixer fitted with a dough hook running at medium-low speed, until all the ingredients are fully incorporated.

Ferment: Form the dough into a ball, then place it in a 4-cup (1-L) proofing bowl. Cover the bowl with its lid and place it in the oven with the light on. Let the dough rest for 30 to 60 minutes, or until the dough begins to rise a little. Place the covered bowl in the fridge overnight for the bulk fermentation.

(continued)

Pumpkin-Chai *Bread* (continued)

Loaf (cont.)

30 g olive oil

23 g whole psyllium husk

130 g pumpkin puree

White rice flour, as needed

Shape: The next day, remove the dough from the fridge and leave it at room temperature for about 30 minutes, until it is warm enough to work with. Liberally dust a 7-inch (18-cm) banneton with the white rice flour. Lightly dampen a work surface with water. Transfer the dough to the prepared work surface. Knead the dough with wet hands for 2 to 3 minutes, and then shape it into a ball. Sprinkle a little white rice flour on the dough's surface, then repeat the kneading process for about 1 minute. With cupped hands, drag the dough in small circles to shape it into a smooth ball. Pinch, seal and smooth any seams in the dough. Scoop the dough up with a bench scraper and gently place it seam side up in the prepared banneton.

Proof: Place the dough, still in the banneton, inside a reusable plastic bag and let it rest at room temperature—ideally about 72°F (22°C)—for 3 to 5 hours. The proofing time depends on the temperature of your kitchen. If the temperature is a little colder, place the dough in the oven with the light on. In the summer warmth, it can be left on the counter, and it may benefit from less proofing time. When the dough has proofed enough, it will have risen and will feel soft, puffy and spongy on the sides and in the center. Chill the dough in the refrigerator for 30 minutes before baking it to create a little more oven spring.

Score: If you will be baking the bread in a Dutch oven, preheat the oven to 450°F (232°C) with a Dutch oven inside. Meanwhile, cut out some parchment paper for the dough to sit on. Place the parchment paper on top of the dough, which should still be in the banneton. Flip the banneton upside down, so that the parchment paper is underneath to hold the dough, and remove the banneton. To create a pumpkin-shaped loaf, cut five pieces of baking string that are long enough to wrap underneath the dough with enough excess to tie the ends together on the top of the dough. Lightly dampen the surface of the dough with wet fingers. Sprinkle some white rice flour on the dough, then evenly spread the flour around the top of the dough with your hands. Tie the strings together with a little tension at the 12 o'clock position on the dough. Cut off any excess string. Score a shallow leaf design between each section of string.

Bake: Gently slide the paper with the dough into the Dutch oven. Cover the Dutch oven with its lid and bake the loaf for 25 minutes. Remove the Dutch oven's lid, reduce the oven's temperature to 400°F (204°C) and bake the loaf for 35 minutes. Reduce the oven's temperature to 350°F (177°C) and remove the loaf from the Dutch oven. Place the loaf on the oven's center rack and bake it for 10 minutes, or until the loaf feels firm.

Place the hot sourdough on a wire rack for at least 2 hours before removing the string and slicing the bread.

Wrap the bread in a tea towel or beeswax wraps and store it on the counter for 2 to 3 days. If your sourdough begins to dry out too quickly, it is best to slice and freeze the remainder. The sourdough will last in the freezer for up to 3 months.

Potato *and* Chive Bread

When you shape the dough for this bread, the texture feels light, fluffy and cloudlike. This is my favorite savory bread in this book, perhaps because of the potatoes, or maybe because of the chives—but either way, the flavors work so well together. I know you will love this bread too!

Note that new and baby potatoes will not work well for this recipe.

Makes 1 loaf

Levain

50 g active starter

100 g warm water

50 g buckwheat flour

50 g brown rice flour

Loaf

125 g russet potato (1 large potato), peeled and quartered

70 g tapioca starch

50 g sorghum flour

50 g buckwheat flour

40 g millet flour

30 g oat flour

15 g granulated sugar

10 g salt

20 g melted butter

¼ tsp black pepper

3 g finely chopped fresh chives

4 g flaxseed, finely ground

22 g whole psyllium husk

310 g potato cooking water

White rice flour, as needed

Reactivate your starter the day before you plan on building the levain. A good time to do this is when you get up in the morning, to allow the starter 6 to 8 hours to become bubbly and active. You will need 50 grams for the levain and at least 20 grams left over for maintaining your original starter/main culture (see page 14 for more information on the feeding ratio).

Build the levain: Using a kitchen scale, weigh 50 grams of active starter in a clean 750-milliliter jar. Add 100 grams of warm water and vigorously whisk the starter and water together. Add 50 grams of buckwheat flour and 50 grams of brown rice flour. Ferment the levain for 6 to 8 hours, or until it is bubbly and it has risen to a peak, before mixing it into the dough.

Mix the dough: In a medium saucepan, cover the quartered potato with water. Bring the potato to a boil over high heat. Reduce the heat to low, cover the saucepan and cook the potato until it is just tender. Drain the potato, reserving 310 grams of the potato cooking water in a medium bowl and adding some fresh water if there isn't enough cooking water to reserve. Return the potato to the saucepan.

In a large bowl, combine the tapioca starch, sorghum flour, buckwheat flour, millet flour, oat flour, granulated sugar and salt. Weigh the cooked and cooled potato. In the saucepan, mash the potato with the butter, and then mix in the black pepper and chives. Sprinkle the flaxseed and psyllium husk on top of the reserved potato water and whisk it immediately to prevent lumps from forming. Mix the levain with the water, flaxseed and psyllium husk, and then mix in the mashed potato. Add the potato mixture to the flour blend. Mix the dough well by hand, or with a kitchen mixer fitted with a dough hook running at medium-low speed, until all the ingredients are fully incorporated.

Ferment: Form the dough into a ball, then place it in a 4-cup (1-L) proofing bowl. Cover the bowl with its lid and place it in the oven with the light on. Let the dough rest for 30 to 60 minutes, or until the dough begins to rise a little. Place the covered bowl in the fridge overnight for the bulk fermentation.

Shape: The next day, remove the dough from the fridge and leave it at room temperature for about 30 minutes, until it is warm enough to work with. Liberally dust a 7-inch (18-cm) banneton with the white rice flour. Lightly dampen a work surface with water. Transfer the dough to the prepared work surface. Knead the dough with wet hands for 2 to 3 minutes, and then shape it into a ball. Sprinkle a little white rice flour on the dough's surface, then repeat the kneading process for about 1 minute. With cupped hands, drag the dough in small circles to shape it into a smooth ball. Pinch, seal and smooth any seams in the dough. Scoop the dough up with a bench scraper and gently place it seam side up in the prepared banneton.

Proof: Place the dough, still in the banneton, inside a reusable plastic bag and let it rest at room temperature—ideally about 72°F (22°C)—for 3 to 5 hours. The proofing time depends on the temperature of your kitchen. If the temperature is a little colder, place the dough in the oven with the light on. In the summer warmth, it can be left on the counter, and it may benefit from less proofing time. When the dough has proofed enough, it will have risen and will feel soft, puffy and spongy on the sides and in the center. Chill the dough in the refrigerator for 30 minutes before baking it to create a little more oven spring.

Score: If you will be baking the bread in a Dutch oven, preheat the oven to 450°F (232°C) with a Dutch oven inside. Meanwhile, cut out some parchment paper for the dough to sit on. Place the parchment paper on top of the dough, which should still be in the banneton. Flip the banneton upside down, so that the parchment paper is underneath to hold the dough, and remove the banneton. Lightly dampen the surface of the dough with wet fingers. Sprinkle some white rice flour on the dough, then evenly spread the flour around the top of the dough with your hands. Score three diagonal lines on top of the dough and down the dough's length.

Bake: Gently slide the parchment paper with the dough into the Dutch oven. Cover the Dutch oven with its lid and bake the loaf for 25 minutes. Reduce the oven's temperature to 425°F (218°C), remove the Dutch oven's lid and bake the loaf for 30 to 35 minutes. Reduce the heat once more to 400°F (204°C) and remove the bread from the Dutch oven. Place the bread directly on the oven rack and bake it for 10 minutes to further brown and crisp the crust. There should be no soft or undercooked areas when you poke the bread with your fingers.

Place the hot sourdough on a wire rack for at least 2 hours before slicing the bread.

Wrap the bread in a tea towel or beeswax wraps and store it on the counter for 2 to 3 days. If your sourdough begins to dry out too quickly, it is best to slice and freeze the remainder. The sourdough will last in the freezer for up to 3 months.

See image on page 52.

bagels, baguettes *and* bites

Even though celiac disease is a lifelong diagnosis, it does not mean you need to live life without amazing bakery and coffee shop goodies. Remember when it was so easy to walk into those places and choose anything you wanted, before any dietary restrictions? This selection of gluten-free sourdough breads is just like having a specialty bakery in your own home! What a treat to finally be able to eat some of these favorites again.

Many of these delectable small breads are best served warm from the oven, but they also reheat well. The Ciabatta Buns (page 79) make for the best grilled sandwiches, and it's liberating to be able to eat fresh Easy Bagels (page 82) for breakfast once more.

Sesame Dinner Rolls

Enjoy fresh-from-the-oven, light, soft dinner rolls once more. Many store-bought gluten-free rolls are not light and fluffy, and before I started making these rolls, I would have gone without the bread. There are so many ways to eat these dinner rolls—they are equally as good warm from the oven or cold the next day. The delicious aroma of freshly baked dinner rolls brings back childhood memories of cold, rainy nights and the warmth of my mother's kitchen. Breaking off pieces of bread to mop up the last bits of tasty stew at the bottom of my bowl is comforting to me and keeps me connected to my past.

This recipe requires two levain feedings.

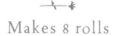

Makes 8 rolls

Morning Levain Feeding

30 g active starter

60 g warm water

30 g brown rice flour

30 g buckwheat flour

Afternoon Levain Feeding

150 g levain from the morning feeding

140 g warm water

40 g brown rice flour

30 g buckwheat flour

20 g quinoa flour

Reactivate your starter the day before you plan on building the levain. A good time to do this is right before bed, to allow the starter 6 to 8 hours to become bubbly and active. You will need 30 grams for the levain and at least 20 grams left over for maintaining your original starter/main culture (see page 14 for more information on the feeding ratio).

Build the levain: For the morning levain feeding, use a kitchen scale to weigh 30 grams of active starter in a clean 750-milliliter jar. Vigorously whisk in 60 grams of warm water, then add 30 grams of brown rice flour and 30 grams of buckwheat flour.

For the afternoon levain feeding, to the same jar with 150 grams of active starter (all of the morning's levain), add 140 grams of warm water, 40 grams of brown rice flour, 30 grams of buckwheat flour and 20 grams of quinoa flour, whisking the ingredients vigorously.

Mix the dough: In a large bowl, combine the brown rice flour, millet flour, oat flour, quinoa flour, sorghum flour, tapioca starch, sugar and salt. In a medium bowl, combine the warm water, warm milk, olive oil and egg. Stir in the psyllium husk. Whisk this mixture immediately to prevent lumps from forming, then whisk in the levain and add this mixture to the flour blend. Mix the dough well by hand, or with a kitchen mixer fitted with a dough hook running at medium-low speed, until all the ingredients are fully incorporated.

(continued)

Sesame Dinner Rolls (continued)

Rolls

84 g brown rice flour

50 g millet flour

56 g oat flour

30 g quinoa flour

84 g sorghum flour

90 g tapioca starch

20 g granulated sugar

11 g salt

165 g warm water

140 g warm milk

15 g olive oil

1 large egg, at room temperature

21 g whole psyllium husk

White rice flour, as needed

10 g sesame seeds

Glaze

15 g honey

15 g soy sauce

5 g olive oil or sesame seed oil

Ferment: Form the dough into a ball, then place it in a 4-cup (1-L) proofing bowl. Cover the bowl with its lid and place it in the oven with the light on. Let the dough rest for 30 to 60 minutes, or until the dough begins to rise a little. Place the covered bowl in the fridge overnight for the bulk fermentation.

Shape: The next day, remove the dough from the fridge and leave it at room temperature for 30 minutes, until it is warm enough to work with. Place a heavy tea towel on 2 medium baking sheets, then create four valleys on each baking sheet by pulling the cloth up to form rows (like an accordion pleat) for the dough to rise in. Place a strip of parchment paper at the bottom of each valley. Lightly dampen a work surface. Transfer the dough to the prepared work surface. Knead the dough with wet hands for 2 to 3 minutes, until it is somewhat smooth. Cut it into eight portions of about 145 grams each. Shape each piece of dough into an oval roll about the size of an avocado, using a small amount of flour to create a smooth surface. Place the dough in the valleys on the baking sheets.

Proof: Cover the dough with a damp tea towel and let it rest at room temperature—ideally about 72°F (22°C)—for 3 to 5 hours. The proofing time depends on the temperature of your kitchen. If the temperature is a little colder, place the dough in the oven with the light on. In the summer warmth, it can be left on the counter, and it may benefit from less proofing time. When the dough has proofed enough, it will have risen and will feel soft, puffy and spongy on the sides and in the center. Chill the dough in the refrigerator for 30 minutes before baking it to create a little more oven spring.

Score: Preheat the oven to 450°F (232°C) with a large pizza stone inside. Meanwhile, cut out some parchment paper to fit the pizza stone and carefully place the rolls on the parchment paper. With wet hands, lightly dampen the surface of the dough and dust some white rice flour on the tops of the rolls. Score a shallow line down the center of each roll and sprinkle the tops with the sesame seeds.

Bake: Gently slide the paper with the dough onto the hot pizza stone and bake the rolls for 12 minutes. Reduce the oven's temperature to 400°F (204°C) and bake the rolls for 10 minutes, until they are golden brown and feel firm to the touch.

Make the glaze: In a small bowl, combine the honey, soy sauce and olive oil. Turn off the oven and brush the rolls with the glaze. Leave the rolls in the oven for 5 minutes to allow the glaze to set, then transfer the rolls to a wire rack to cool slightly. These rolls are best enjoyed while they are still warm.

Wrap the rolls in a tea towel or beeswax wraps and store them on the counter for up to 2 days. The rolls can be frozen for up to 3 months.

Ciabatta Buns

With a light golden crust, these gluten-free buns are soft, delicious and form into an elongated shape similar to a slipper, which is what ciabatta translates to in Italian. This high-hydration dough creates an incredible open bread crumb (i.e., larger holes in the bread) to provide light and airy buns. Pictures of regular sourdough on Instagram or in recipe books tend to show stunning open-crumb breads, but with gluten-free bread, this is harder to achieve without the structure gluten provides—which is another reason why these buns are so unique.

Grill the buns to create a delicious hot panini sandwich with your favorite fillings. You can reheat the ciabatta buns in the oven at 350°F (177°C) for ten minutes to restore that freshly baked goodness and crispy crust.

This recipe requires two levain feedings.

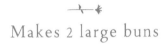

Makes 2 large buns

Morning Levain Feeding

25 g active starter

50 g warm water

25 g buckwheat flour

25 g brown rice flour

Afternoon Levain Feeding

125 g levain from the morning feeding

140 g warm water

50 g buckwheat flour

50 g sweet white rice flour

Buns

30 g buckwheat flour

40 g tapioca starch

35 g potato starch

50 g sweet white rice flour

40 g brown rice flour

40 g millet flour

Reactivate your starter the day before you plan on building the levain. A good time to do this is right before bed, to allow the starter 6 to 8 hours to become bubbly and active. You will need 25 grams for the levain and at least 20 grams left over for maintaining your original starter/main culture (see page 14 for more information on the feeding ratio).

Build the levain: For the morning levain feeding, use a kitchen scale to weigh 25 grams of active starter in a clean 750-milliliter jar. Vigorously whisk in 50 grams of warm water, then add 25 grams of buckwheat flour and 25 grams of brown rice flour.

For the afternoon levain feeding, in the same jar with 125 grams of active starter (all of the morning's levain), vigorously whisk in 140 grams of warm water. Add 50 grams of buckwheat flour and 50 grams of sweet white rice flour. Ferment the second levain for 6 to 8 hours, or until it is bubbly and has risen to a peak, before mixing it into the dough.

Mix the dough: In a large bowl, combine the buckwheat flour, tapioca starch, potato starch, sweet white rice flour, brown rice flour, millet flour, oat flour, sugar, Italian seasoning and salt. In a medium bowl, beat together the egg, levain and olive oil for about 1 minute, until the mixture is aerated and bubbly looking. Gently beat in the warm water. Stir the psyllium husk into the levain mixture to create a gel. Immediately whisk everything well to prevent lumps from forming. Pour the psyllium gel into the flour blend. Mix the dough well by hand, or with a kitchen mixer fitted with a dough hook running at medium-low speed, until all the ingredients are fully incorporated. Since this recipe forms a soft, sticky dough, it is easier to mix it with a kitchen mixer fitted with a dough hook. If you use your hands, keep them wet to prevent the dough from sticking to them.

(continued)

Ciabatta *Buns* (continued)

Buns (cont.)

20 g oat flour

5 g granulated sugar

⅛ tsp Italian seasoning

8 g salt

1 large egg, at room temperature

15 g olive oil

225 g warm water

18 g whole psyllium husk

White rice flour, as needed

Ferment: Form the dough into a ball, then place it in a 4-cup (1-L) proofing bowl. Cover the bowl with its lid and place it in the oven with the light on. Let the dough rest for 30 to 60 minutes, or until the dough begins to rise a little. Place the covered bowl in the fridge overnight for the bulk fermentation.

Shape: The next day, remove the dough from the fridge and leave it at room temperature for about 30 minutes, until it is warm enough to work with. Place a heavy tea towel on a medium baking sheet, then create two valleys by pulling the cloth up to form rows (like an accordion pleat) for the dough to rise in. Place a strip of parchment paper at the bottom of each valley. Lightly dampen a work surface with water. Transfer the dough to the prepared work surface. Knead the dough with a small amount of white rice flour for 2 to 3 minutes. Divide the dough in half, then shape each half to form a 4 x 8–inch (10 x 20–cm) rectangle with slightly rounded corners. Place the dough in the tea towel valleys.

Proof: Cover the dough with a damp tea towel and let it rest at room temperature—ideally about 72°F (22°C)—for 3 to 5 hours. The proofing time depends on the temperature of your kitchen. If the temperature is a little colder, place the dough in the oven with the light on. In the summer warmth, it can be left on the counter, and it may benefit from less proofing time. When the dough has proofed enough, it will have risen and will feel soft, puffy and spongy on the sides and in the center. Chill the dough in the refrigerator for 30 minutes before baking it to create a little more oven spring.

Bake: Preheat the oven to 450°F (232°C) with a large pizza stone on the center rack. Slide the parchment paper with the dough onto the hot pizza stone and immediately reduce the oven's temperature to 400°F (204°C). Bake the buns for 25 minutes, then reduce the oven's temperature to 350°F (177°C). Bake the buns for 10 minutes, until they are firm to the touch and lightly browned.

Place the buns on a wire rack for at least 2 hours to cool.

Wrap the buns in a tea towel or beeswax wraps and store them on the counter for up to 2 days. The buns can be frozen for up to 3 months.

Easy Bagels

These are not store-bought gluten-free bagels—they're so much better! They're just like
the ones I ate before I went gluten-free. Whether you like a plain bagel, an everything bagel or
a sweet cinnamon-raisin twist bagel, you are free to choose with this adaptable recipe.
My favorite is a warm toasted seeded bagel slathered in cream cheese and topped with
crunchy cucumber slices that have been sprinkled with salt and pepper.

Boiling the bagels sets the crust, and the bagels will puff up nicely in the water bath.
In this recipe, I use a baking soda bath. You can choose to create that glossy, golden-brown finish
with an egg wash, and you can add sesame seeds or other toppings. It is so easy to grab bagels from
a store, but the difference in taste with these homemade bagels is unparalleled, and thankfully
bagels are one of the easiest breads to make at home.

— ✦ —

Makes 8 bagels

Levain

45 g active starter

90 g warm water

45 g buckwheat flour

30 g brown rice flour

15 g millet flour

Bagels

50 g potato starch

30 g tapioca starch

75 g brown rice flour

50 g buckwheat flour

45 g millet flour

9 g salt

150 g warm water

150 g cold milk

30 g cold butter

20 g whole psyllium husk

8 g flaxseed, finely ground

White rice flour, as needed

45 g baking soda

Olive oil or whisked egg white,
as needed

Reactivate your starter the day before you plan on building the levain. A good time to
do this is when you get up in the morning, to allow the starter 6 to 8 hours to become
bubbly and active. You will need 45 grams for the levain and at least 20 grams left over
for maintaining your original starter/main culture (see page 14 for more information on
the feeding ratio).

Build the levain: Using a kitchen scale, weigh 45 grams of active starter in a clean
750-milliliter jar. Vigorously mix in 90 grams of warm water, then add 45 grams of
buckwheat flour, 30 grams of brown rice flour and 15 grams of millet flour. Ferment the
levain for 6 to 8 hours, or until it is bubbly and has risen to a peak, before mixing it into
the dough.

Mix the dough: In a large bowl, combine the potato starch, tapioca starch, brown rice
flour, buckwheat flour, millet flour and salt. In a medium saucepan over medium-low
heat, combine the warm water, cold milk and butter, and warm the mixture until the
butter is just melted. Allow the mixture to cool for about 10 minutes, until it is lukewarm.
Stir the psyllium husk and flaxseed into the cooled mixture and immediately whisk the
ingredients to prevent lumps from forming. Whisk the levain into the psyllium mixture,
then add the mixture to the flour blend. Mix the dough well by hand, or with a kitchen
mixer fitted with a dough hook running at medium-low speed, until all the ingredients
are fully incorporated.

Ferment: Form the dough into a ball, then place it in a 4-cup (1-L) proofing bowl. Cover
the bowl with its lid and place it in the oven with the light on. Let the dough rest for
30 to 60 minutes, or until the dough begins to rise a little. Place the covered bowl in the
fridge overnight for the bulk fermentation.

(continued)

Easy Bagels (continued)

Suggested Toppings

Everything seasoning

Cinnamon sugar and raisins

Salt

Hemp seeds

Poppy seeds

Sesame seeds

Shape: The next day, remove the dough from the fridge and leave it on the counter for about 30 minutes, until it is warm enough to work with. Line a large baking sheet with parchment paper. Lightly dampen a work surface with water. Transfer the dough to the prepared work surface. Knead the dough for 2 to 3 minutes with a small amount of white rice flour. Roll the dough into a 10-inch (25-cm)-long log. Slice the log into eight pieces. Poke your finger through each bagel's center, making a hole the size of two fingers, to create the typical bagel shape. Finish shaping the dough with damp hands and place each bagel on the prepared baking sheet.

Proof: Cover the bagels with a damp tea towel and let them rest at room temperature—ideally about 72°F (22°C)—for 3 to 5 hours. The proofing time depends on the temperature of your kitchen. If the temperature is a little colder, place the dough in the oven with the light on. In the summer warmth, it can be left on the counter, and it may benefit from less proofing time. When the dough has proofed enough, it will have risen and will feel soft, puffy and spongy on the sides and in the center.

Water bath: Preheat the oven to 450°F (232°C) with a large pizza stone on the middle rack. Place the baking soda in a small ovenproof skillet. Put the baking soda in the oven to bake for 10 minutes while the oven is preheating. Meanwhile, bring a large pot of water to a boil over high heat, then reduce the heat to medium and bring the water to a gentle simmer. Add the baking soda to the water. Then, carefully put four of the bagels in the water. They will immediately rise to the water's surface. Gently turn each bagel over with tongs before transferring them to a wire cooling rack. Repeat the process with the remaining bagels. Place the bagels back on the parchment paper that they rose on and brush the tops with the olive oil. Sprinkle the bagels with any of the suggested toppings.

Bake: Gently slide the paper with the dough onto the preheated pizza stone and bake the bagels for 10 minutes with the oven temperature still at 450°F (232°C). Reduce the oven's temperature to 375°F (191°C) and bake the bagels for 15 minutes, or until they are lightly browned.

Place the hot bagels on a wire rack to cool for 30 minutes before slicing them.

Wrap the bagels in a tea towel or beeswax wraps and store them on the counter for up to 2 days. If your bagels begin to dry out too quickly, it is best to freeze the remainder. The bagels will last in the freezer for up to 3 months.

Focaccia with Bruschetta *and* Thyme

Even though this focaccia is spread out in a flat pan, with the gluten-free levain it quickly grows into thick and spongy bread that requires little effort. The bruschetta topping is baked into the top of the bread and then sprinkled with fresh, fragrant thyme. If you want to experiment, you can try other kinds of toppings as well. Your options are limitless—some of the most common include garlic, tomatoes, olives, cheese, herbs and peppers. Regardless of the topping you choose, you should try dipping the bread in a little olive oil and balsamic vinegar as you eat it.

Makes 1 pan

Levain

50 g active starter

100 g warm water

50 g buckwheat flour

50 g brown rice flour

Focaccia

30 g oat flour

30 g quinoa flour

50 g buckwheat flour

50 g sorghum flour

40 g tapioca starch

9 g salt

280 g warm water

50 g aquafaba or 1 large egg, at room temperature

20 g olive oil, plus more as needed

16 g whole psyllium husk

Reactivate your starter the day before you plan on building the levain. A good time to do this is when you get up in the morning, to allow the starter 6 to 8 hours to become bubbly and active. You will need 50 grams for the levain and at least 20 grams left over for maintaining your original starter/main culture (see page 14 for more information on the feeding ratio).

Build the levain: Using a kitchen scale, weigh 50 grams of active starter in a clean 750-milliliter jar. Vigorously whisk in 100 grams of warm water, then add 50 grams of buckwheat flour and 50 grams of brown rice flour. Ferment the levain for 6 to 8 hours, or until it is bubbly and has risen to a peak, before mixing it into the dough.

Mix the dough: In a large bowl, combine the oat flour, quinoa flour, buckwheat flour, sorghum flour, tapioca starch and salt. In a medium bowl, combine the warm water, aquafaba and olive oil. Stir in the psyllium husk. Whisk this mixture immediately to prevent lumps from forming, then mix in the levain. Add this mixture to the flour blend. Mix the dough well by hand, or with a kitchen mixer fitted with a dough hook running at medium-low speed, until all the ingredients are fully incorporated.

Ferment: Form the dough into a ball, then place it in a 4-cup (1-L) proofing bowl. Cover the bowl with its lid and place it in the oven with the light on. Let the dough rest for 30 to 60 minutes, or until the dough begins to rise a little. Place the covered bowl in the fridge overnight for the bulk fermentation. Alternatively, you can leave the proofing bowl on the counter for 1 hour and then proceed with the directions, skipping the overnight fermentation.

(continued)

Focaccia with Bruschetta *and* Thyme (continued)

Topping

125 g homemade or store-bought bruschetta

2 g roughly chopped fresh thyme

Cherry tomatoes, halved

½ tsp salt

⅛ tsp black pepper

Shape: The next day, remove the dough from the fridge and leave it at room temperature for 30 minutes, until it is warm enough to work with. Line an 11 x 8-inch (28 x 20–cm) baking pan with parchment paper. Do not knead the dough; rather, shape it into a rough rectangle and place it in the prepared pan. Using your fingers, spread the dough out to the edges of the pan without pressing it too flat. Brush additional olive oil over the top of the dough.

Proof: Cover the dough with a damp tea towel and let it rest at room temperature—ideally about 72°F (22°C)—for 3 to 5 hours. The proofing time depends on the temperature of your kitchen. If the temperature is a little colder, place the dough in the oven with the light on. In the summer warmth, it can be left on the counter, and it may benefit from less proofing time. When the dough has proofed enough, it will have risen and will feel soft, puffy and spongy on the sides and in the center. Lightly dimple the top of the dough with your fingertips.

Bake: Preheat the oven to 450°F (232°C). Meanwhile, create the bread's topping by spreading the bruschetta on top of the dough and sprinkling the thyme on the bruschetta. Place the baking pan with the focaccia on the oven's middle rack and bake it for 15 minutes. Reduce the oven's temperature to 400°F (204°C) and bake the focaccia for 25 to 30 minutes, until the top is golden brown and the dough is firm to the touch.

Place the hot sourdough on a wire rack to cool for 20 minutes before slicing it. Top each slice with the cherry tomatoes and season the tomatoes with the salt and black pepper.

Serve this bread while it is still warm. Leftovers will keep, stored on the counter in the covered baking pan, until the next day.

Fougasse with Tzatziki *and* Dill

Fougasse is a French flatbread often topped with spices and herbs and shaped to look like a leaf. This delicious, crisp-crusted bread makes a tasty appetizer with a glass of wine, or it can be served as an accompaniment with soups and stews. You can experiment with different leaf shapes, herbs and toppings! All you need is a bread lame or a sharp, fine-point knife to make one large leaf or a couple of smaller ones.

—⊹—⋆

Makes 1 large fougasse or 2 small fougasses

Levain

30 g active starter

60 g warm water

30 g buckwheat flour

30 g brown rice flour

Fougasse

50 g buckwheat flour

65 g tapioca starch

30 g sweet white rice flour

70 g brown rice flour

30 g millet flour

10 g salt

⅛ tsp Italian seasoning

230 g warm water

40 g olive oil, plus more as needed

20 g whole psyllium husk

Reactivate your starter the day before you plan on building the levain. A good time to do this is when you get up in the morning, to allow the starter 6 to 8 hours to become bubbly and active. You will need 30 grams for the levain and at least 20 grams left over for maintaining your original starter/main culture (see page 14 for more information on the feeding ratio).

Build the levain: Using a kitchen scale, weigh 30 grams of active starter in a clean 750-milliliter jar. Vigorously whisk in 60 grams of warm water, then add 30 grams of buckwheat flour and 30 grams of brown rice flour. Ferment the levain for 6 to 8 hours, or until it is bubbly and has risen to a peak, before mixing it into the dough.

Mix the dough: In a large bowl, combine the buckwheat flour, tapioca starch, sweet white rice flour, brown rice flour, millet flour, salt and Italian seasoning. In a medium bowl, combine the warm water and olive oil. Stir in the psyllium husk. Whisk the mixture immediately to prevent lumps from forming, then mix in the levain. Add the levain mixture to the flour blend. Mix the dough well by hand, or with a kitchen mixer fitted with a dough hook running at medium-low speed, until all the ingredients are fully incorporated.

Ferment: Form the dough into a ball, then place it in a 4-cup (1-L) proofing bowl. Cover the bowl with its lid and place it in the oven with the light on. Let the dough rest for 30 to 60 minutes, or until the dough begins to rise a little. Place the covered bowl in the fridge overnight for the bulk fermentation. Alternatively, you can leave this dough on the counter for the night. It is a stiffer dough and takes longer to rise.

Shape: The next day, remove the dough from the fridge and leave it at room temperature for 30 minutes, until it is warm enough to work with. Line a large baking sheet with parchment paper. Lightly dampen a work surface with water. Transfer the dough to the prepared work surface. Knead the dough with wet hands for 2 to 3 minutes, then transfer it to the prepared baking sheet. Stretch and shape the dough into a large leaf shape with damp hands, then with a bread lame or shape knife, cut a long slash down the center of the dough to resemble a leaf vein, cutting completely through the dough and opening up the slash a little. Do not cut through each end. Then, cut three or four smaller slits on each side of the center at a diagonal angle to represent smaller veins. Alternatively, you can split the dough in half and make two smaller leaves.

(continued)

Fougasse with Tzatziki *and* Dill (continued)

Topping

60 g homemade or store-bought tzatziki

1 g fresh dill

Proof: Cover the dough with a damp tea towel and let it rest at room temperature—ideally about 72°F (22°C)—for 2 to 3 hours. The proofing time depends on the temperature of your kitchen. If the temperature is a little colder, place the dough in the oven with the light on. In the summer warmth, it can be left on the counter, and it may benefit from less proofing time. When the dough has proofed enough, it will have risen and will feel soft, puffy and spongy on top.

Score: Preheat the oven to 450°F (232°C) with a large pizza stone on the middle rack. Meanwhile, create very fine leaf veins with a bread lame for extra decoration on the top of the dough and around the previous cuts.

Bake: Gently slide the parchment paper with the dough onto the preheated pizza stone and bake the bread for 20 minutes. Reduce the oven's temperature to 400°F (204°C) and bake the bread for 30 to 35 minutes, until it is brown and crispy. To create the bread's topping, during the last 10 minutes of baking, lightly spread the tzatziki on top of the fougasse.

Place the fougasse on a wire rack to cool for 30 minutes. Sprinkle the dill over the top. Serve this bread the same day that you bake it.

Potato English Muffins

This is my favorite bread for breakfast sandwiches—it is half sourdough and half hash brown! It reminds me of those fast-food breakfast sandwiches that I used to eat before I was diagnosed with celiac disease. Slice the bun in half, toast it in a skillet, cook up an egg in the same rings that you baked the buns in and it is a perfect fit. Add any extra fillings and repeat the next day!

Note that when you cook the potatoes, you need to save the potato cooking water for the dough. Also, for this recipe, you will need ten 3½-inch (9-cm) English muffin rings.

This recipe requires two levain feedings.

—✦—

Makes 10 muffins

Morning Levain Feeding

25 g active starter

50 g warm water

25 g brown rice flour

25 g buckwheat flour

Afternoon Levain Feeding

125 g levain from the morning feeding

130 g warm water

30 g brown rice flour

30 g buckwheat flour

Muffins

50 g potato starch

40 g buckwheat flour

30 g millet flour

8 g salt

¼ tsp black pepper

130 g whole peeled and cooked russet potato

Reactivate your starter the day before you plan on building the levain. A good time to do this is right before bed, to allow the starter 6 to 8 hours to become bubbly and active. You will need 25 grams for the levain and at least 20 grams left over for maintaining your original starter/main culture (see page 14 for more information on the feeding ratio).

Build the levain: For the morning levain feeding, use a kitchen scale to weigh 25 grams of active starter in a clean 750-milliliter jar. Vigorously whisk in 50 grams of warm water, then add 25 grams of brown rice flour and 25 grams of buckwheat flour.

For the afternoon levain feeding, in the same jar with the 125 grams of active starter (all of the morning's levain), vigorously whisk in 130 grams of water. Add 30 grams of brown rice flour and 30 grams of buckwheat flour. Ferment the levain for 6 to 8 hours, or until it is bubbly and has risen to a peak, before mixing it into the dough.

Mix the dough: In a large bowl, combine the potato starch, buckwheat flour, millet flour, salt and black pepper. In a small blender, blend together the cooked potato, egg and butter until the mixture reaches a smooth consistency. Transfer the potato mixture to a medium bowl. Add the potato cooking water to the potato mixture. Whisk in the psyllium husk and flaxseed to create a gel. Whisk this gel mixture immediately to prevent lumps from forming, then mix in the levain. Add this mixture to the flour blend. Mix the dough well by hand, or with a kitchen mixer fitted with a dough hook running at medium-low speed, until all the ingredients are fully incorporated.

Ferment: Grease ten 3½-inch (9-cm) English muffin rings. Line a large baking sheet with parchment paper, then place the English muffin rings on the prepared baking sheet. Fill each ring evenly with the dough, so that the dough fills the rings completely. Smooth the tops of the muffins with a spatula. Cover the whole baking sheet with plastic wrap and leave the dough to rise for 6 to 8 hours, until it is nearly to the top of the rings. If your house is cooler than 68°F (20°C), the muffins can ferment overnight.

(continued)

Potato English Muffins (continued)

Muffins (cont.)

1 large egg, at room temperature

30 g melted butter

120 g potato cooking water

12 g whole psyllium husk

4 g flaxseed, finely ground

Bake: Preheat the oven to 425°F (218°C) and bake the muffins for 15 minutes. Reduce the oven's temperature to 375°F (191°C) and bake the muffins for 15 minutes, until they are firm on top and light brown.

Place the hot muffins on a wire rack to cool for at least 2 hours.

Wrap the muffins in a tea towel or beeswax wraps and store them on the counter for up to 3 days. In a sealed bag in the fridge, these muffins will keep for 7 to 10 days, and they reheat very well. They will last in the freezer for up to 3 months.

Same-Day Baguettes

Here is an easy and delicious bread that is the perfect accompaniment to any cheese plate or charcuterie board. You can also use these baguettes to make fresh oven-baked crostini to use with appetizers. Slice the bread about ½ inch (1.3 cm) thick and toast it in a 400°F (204°C) oven for ten minutes, until crisp.

—⊹—⊱

Makes 2 baguettes

Levain

25 g active starter

50 g warm water

25 g brown rice flour

25 g buckwheat flour

Baguettes

50 g white rice flour, plus more as needed

50 g brown rice flour

40 g millet flour

10 g teff flour

50 g sorghum flour

50 g cornstarch

1 tsp finely chopped fresh thyme

5 g salt

1 large egg, at room temperature

30 g honey

300 g warm water

20 g whole psyllium husk

Olive oil, as needed

1 large clove garlic, halved

Reactivate your starter the day before you plan on building the levain. A good time to do this is when you get up in the morning, to allow the starter 6 to 8 hours to become bubbly and active. You will need 25 grams for the levain and at least 20 grams left over for maintaining your original starter/main culture (see page 14 for more information on the feeding ratio).

Build the levain: Using a kitchen scale, weigh 25 grams of active starter in a clean 500-milliliter jar. Vigorously mix in 50 grams of warm water, then add 25 grams of brown rice flour and 25 grams of buckwheat flour. Ferment the levain for 6 to 8 hours, or until it is bubbly and has risen to a peak, before mixing it into the dough.

Mix the dough: In a large bowl, combine the white rice flour, brown rice flour, millet flour, teff flour, sorghum flour, cornstarch, thyme and salt. In a medium bowl, lightly beat the egg. Add the honey, warm water and levain and beat the ingredients until they are just combined. Beat the psyllium husk into the egg mixture. Add the egg mixture to the flour blend. Mix the dough well by hand, or with a kitchen mixer fitted with a dough hook running at medium-low speed, until all the ingredients are fully incorporated.

Ferment: Form the dough into a ball, then place it in a 4-cup (1-L) proofing bowl. Cover the bowl with its lid and let the dough rise for 2 to 3 hours in a warm place.

Shape: Place a heavy tea towel on a large baking sheet. Create two valleys that are 2½ inches (6 cm) wide by pulling the cloth up to form rows (like an accordion pleat) for the dough to rise in. Cut two strips of parchment paper that are slightly larger than each valley, then place a piece of parchment paper in each valley. Lightly dust a work surface with additional white rice flour. Transfer the dough to the prepared work surface. Cut the dough into two 415-gram pieces. Gently roll each piece of dough into a tube that is 2½ inches (6 cm) wide and about 11 inches (28 cm) long and place them in the parchment paper valleys. Alternatively, you can use a baguette pan to maintain a baguette shape.

(continued)

Same-Day Baguettes (continued)

Proof: Cover the dough with a damp tea towel or plastic wrap. Let the dough rest for 2 to 4 hours before baking it. Keep a close eye on the dough, as it will overproof very quickly: It will rise up and become very soft, and it is best to bake it before it starts to flatten on top. Chill the dough in the refrigerator for 30 minutes before baking it, as doing so will help it hold its shape in the oven.

Score: Preheat the oven to 450°F (232°C) with a large pizza stone on the oven's middle rack. Use a sharp knife or bread lame to gently score the baguette with three or four diagonal lines. Do not cut too deeply or you may deflate the dough.

Bake: Bake the baguettes for 25 minutes. Brush some olive oil on the top of each baguette and reduce the oven's temperature to 400°F (204°C). Bake the baguettes for 15 minutes. Reduce the oven's temperature again to 350°F (177°C), remove the baguettes from the parchment paper and bake them directly on the oven rack for 10 minutes, or until they feel firm and are brown on the outside.

Place the hot baguettes on a wire rack to cool. While they are still warm, rub the surface of each of the baguettes with half of the garlic and brush them with a little olive oil. Or enjoy them plain, dipped in olive oil and balsamic vinegar. Let the baguettes cool for 1 hour before slicing them.

Wrap the baguettes in a tea towel or beeswax wraps and store them on the counter for 2 to 3 days. If your baguettes begin to dry out too quickly, it is best to slice and freeze the remainder. The baguettes will last in the freezer for up to 3 months.

$\mathcal{Soft}$ Pretzels

These delicious pretzels are so easy to make, and they boast a golden-brown crust and light, springy center. Although the pretzels are rolled one at a time, this recipe does not take too long because it uses baking soda that has been baked in the oven—there is no dangerous lye used for the water bath.

—◆—

Makes 10 pretzels

Levain

25 g active starter

50 g warm water

25 g brown rice flour

25 g buckwheat flour

Pretzels

65 g tapioca starch

60 g oat flour

45 g sorghum flour

30 g cornstarch

50 g brown rice flour

10 g salt

140 g cold milk

150 g cold water

20 g pure maple syrup

30 g butter, at room temperature

16 g whole psyllium husk

8 g flaxseed, finely ground

White rice flour, as needed

Reactivate your starter the day before you plan on building the levain. A good time to do this is when you get up in the morning, to allow the starter 6 to 8 hours to become bubbly and active. You will need 25 grams for the levain and at least 20 grams left over for maintaining your original starter/main culture (see page 14 for more information on the feeding ratio).

Build the levain: Using a kitchen scale, weigh 25 grams of active starter in a clean 500-milliliter jar. Vigorously mix in the 50 grams of warm water, then add the 25 grams of brown rice flour and 25 grams of buckwheat flour. Ferment the levain for 6 to 8 hours, or until it is bubbly and has risen to a peak, before mixing it into the dough.

Mix the dough: In a large bowl, combine the tapioca starch, oat flour, sorghum flour, cornstarch, brown rice flour and salt. In a medium saucepan over medium-low heat, combine the cold milk, cold water, maple syrup and butter. Warm this mixture just until the butter is melted. Let the mixture cool until it is lukewarm, and then stir in the psyllium husk and flaxseed. Whisk this mixture immediately to prevent lumps from forming, then mix in the levain. Add the mixture to the flour blend. Mix the dough well by hand, or with a kitchen mixer fitted with a dough hook running at medium-low speed, until all the ingredients are fully incorporated.

Ferment: Form the dough into a ball, then place it in a 4-cup (1-L) proofing bowl. Cover the bowl with its lid and place it in the oven with the light on. Let the dough rest for 30 to 60 minutes, or until the dough begins to rise a little. Place the covered bowl in the fridge overnight for the bulk fermentation.

(continued)

Soft Pretzels (continued)

Topping

45 g baking soda
1 large egg, beaten (optional)
5 to 10 g coarse salt

Shape: The next day, remove the dough from the fridge and leave it at room temperature for 30 minutes, until it is warm enough to work with. Line a large baking sheet with parchment paper. Lightly dampen a work surface with water. Transfer the dough to the prepared work surface. Knead the dough with wet hands for 2 to 3 minutes, and then form it into a rough rectangle. With a bench scraper and a kitchen scale, cut and weigh ten 70-gram strips—note that the weight is more important than the shape at this stage because you will roll the dough strips to the same length. Cover half of the dough strips with a damp tea towel while you work with the other half of the strips. With wet hands, roll each strip of dough until it is 16 to 18 inches (40 to 45 cm) long. If the dough is sticky, dust it with the white rice flour. Keep the middle of the dough strip slightly thicker and let the strip taper off to thinner ends. Use a little white rice flour if needed to prevent the dough sticking to your hands, but otherwise just roll the dough with wet hands. Hold the ends of the dough strip up in the air and twist the dough twice to make the pretzel knot. Keep in mind that if the dough strip is too thin, it will break. Gently press the ends down onto the dough to form the classic pretzel shape. You may need wet fingers to attach the ends to the dough. Transfer each pretzel to the prepared baking sheet. Repeat this process with the other half of the dough strips.

Proof: Cover the pretzels with a damp tea towel and let them rest at room temperature—ideally about 72°F (22°C)—for 1 to 2 hours. The proofing time depends on the temperature of your kitchen. If the temperature is a little colder, place the dough in the oven with the light on. In the summer warmth, it can be left on the counter, and it may benefit from less proofing time. When the dough has proofed enough, it will have risen and will feel soft and puffy on the sides and spongy on top.

Water bath: Preheat the oven to 450°F (232°C) with a Dutch oven inside. Bring a large pot of water to a boil over high heat. Meanwhile, place the baking soda in the preheated Dutch oven and bake it for 10 minutes. Once the water is boiling, reduce the heat to medium-low to bring the water to a simmer. Add the baking soda to the water. With a spatula, lower two or three pretzels, one at a time, into the pot. They will begin to float immediately. After 30 seconds, lift them out of the water and place them back on the baking sheet. Repeat this process with the remaining pretzels.

If you would like the pretzels to have a shiny golden-brown finish, brush each pretzel with the beaten egg. Sprinkle the pretzels with the coarse salt.

Bake: With the oven temperature still at 450°F (232°C), bake the pretzels on the baking sheet for about 18 minutes, until they are dark golden brown.

Let the pretzels cool for 5 minutes before serving them. Serve the warm pretzels with your favorite dipping sauce, like a spicy cheese sauce or a honey mustard dip. Store the pretzels in a resealable bag on the counter for 24 hours.

twisted, braided *and* rolled

These beautiful breads with scrumptious fillings can easily be the centerpiece of a meal. This chapter has recipes that are enjoyable to bake and not as challenging as you may think. The trick is to chill the dough for fifteen minutes before shaping these gorgeous braids. When I started my gluten-free journey, I did not believe that this kind of specialty baking with only gluten-free ingredients was possible. That's the beauty of including sourdough in your gluten-free baking: It opens the door to all sorts of delicious baked goods, because it helps bind the dough better than a traditional gluten-free dough.

There are too many delectable recipes in this chapter, so I can't single out a favorite. But I can say you will find it extremely hard to stop eating the Braided Herb and Cheese Loaf (page 102) and the Chocolate and Hazelnut Babka (page 108)!

Braided Herb *and* Cheese Loaf

I have to admit that one evening, after this cheesy, crispy sourdough was baked, I ate half the loaf by myself. This is a full-flavored sourdough with butter, cheese and fresh greens rolled into the center to produce a soft and lightweight bread. Feel free to experiment and use fillings such as fresh garlic tops, sorrel or whatever greens you may be growing. Do not be intimidated by the shaping and braiding of the dough—it's simpler than you think! Just remember to chill the dough before handling it, so it'll be easier to manage. If any of the filling falls out, just push it back in during the final shaping. This is an over-the-top garlic bread with a spectacular look and flavor!

Makes 1 loaf

Levain

25 g active starter

50 g warm water

25 g buckwheat flour

25 g brown rice flour

Loaf

50 g white rice flour, plus more as needed

70 g tapioca starch

65 g sorghum flour

40 g oat flour

25 g buckwheat flour

7 g salt

1 large egg, at room temperature

50 g warm milk

30 g honey

200 g warm water

20 g whole psyllium husk

8 g flaxseed, finely ground

2 g finely chopped fresh dill or 1 tsp dried dill

Reactivate your starter the day before you plan on building the levain. A good time to do this is when you get up in the morning, to allow the starter 6 to 8 hours to become bubbly and active. You will need 25 grams for the levain and at least 20 grams left over for maintaining your original starter/main culture (see page 14 for more information on the feeding ratio).

Build the levain: Using a kitchen scale, weigh 25 grams of active starter in a clean 500-milliliter jar. Vigorously mix in 50 grams of warm water, then add 25 grams of buckwheat flour and 25 grams of brown rice flour. Ferment the levain for 6 to 8 hours, or until it is bubbly and has risen to a peak, before mixing it into the dough.

Mix the dough: In a large bowl, combine the white rice flour, tapioca starch, sorghum flour, oat flour, buckwheat flour and salt. In a medium bowl, beat together the egg, warm milk and honey. Add the warm water to the egg mixture and stir in the psyllium husk and flaxseed. Immediately whisk the mixture to prevent lumps from forming. Add the psyllium mixture to the flour blend, then add the dill. Mix the dough well by hand, or with a kitchen mixer fitted with a dough hook running at medium-low speed, until all the ingredients are fully incorporated.

Ferment: Form the dough into a ball, then place it in a 4-cup (1-L) proofing bowl. Cover the bowl with its lid and place it in the oven with the light on. Let the dough rest for 30 to 60 minutes, or until the dough begins to rise a little. Place the covered bowl in the fridge overnight for the bulk fermentation.

Shape: The next day, remove the dough from the fridge and leave it at room temperature for 30 minutes. Meanwhile, cut a large rectangle of parchment paper and set it aside.

(continued)

Braided Herb *and* Cheese Loaf (continued)

Filling

30 g cold butter

2 cloves garlic, diced

40 g grated Parmesan cheese

40 g grated Gouda cheese

30 g finely chopped spinach

10 g finely chopped fresh parsley

6 g salt

Cut the dough log in half lengthwise.

With the filling facing upward, braid the dough.

Shape the braided dough into a circle and tuck the edges underneath.

To prepare the filling, melt the butter in a small bowl in the microwave. Add the garlic and let the garlic butter cool until it is lukewarm.

Meanwhile, dust a work surface with additional white rice flour, then transfer the dough to the prepared work surface. Knead the dough for 2 to 3 minutes, until it is smooth. Roll out the dough on the parchment paper rectangle until the dough measures 10 x 12 inches (25 x 30 cm). Spread the garlic butter over the entire surface of the dough. Evenly sprinkle the Parmesan cheese and Gouda cheese on top of the butter, then top the cheeses with the spinach and parsley. Roll the dough into a log, making sure to keep the first few rolls tight, but without straining and tearing the dough. Use the parchment paper to help roll the dough tightly. Pinch and seal the edges of the dough log. Tightly wrap the dough in the parchment paper and chill the dough in the refrigerator for 20 minutes to make it easier to braid.

Take the dough log out of the fridge and remove the parchment paper. Place the log on a fresh piece of parchment paper. Cut the dough log in half lengthwise most of the way, leaving about 2 inches (5 cm) uncut at one end and to help with the shaping. Pinch any parts of the dough that try to open too much. Gently turn the halves so that the filling is facing upward, then twist and braid the dough to the end. Cut the uncut end and braid it to match the other end. The dough does not have to be perfectly shaped at this stage. Form a circle with the braided bread, then pinch and seal the edges and tuck them underneath the loaf. Poke back in any filling that falls out and even out the shape of the dough circle with your hands. (See the photos for shaping details.)

Proof: Place the dough, still on the parchment paper, on a medium baking sheet. Put a small shot glass in the center hole of the loaf to hold it open as the dough rises. Grease a medium bowl, then place the bowl upside down over the top of the dough to ensure that it holds its circular shape. Let the dough rest at room temperature—ideally about 72°F (22°C)—for 3 to 5 hours. The proofing time depends on the temperature of your kitchen. If the temperature is a little colder, place the dough in the oven with the light on. Do not let the dough overproof—if it has nearly doubled in height, transfer it to the fridge for the remainder of the proofing time. If the dough proofs at room temperature the entire time, chill the dough in the refrigerator for about 30 minutes prior to baking it, as this will help it keep its shape.

Bake: While the dough is chilling, preheat the oven to 450°F (232°C) with a Dutch oven inside. Remove the shot glass before baking. Carefully slide the parchment paper and dough into the preheated Dutch oven, cover with the lid and bake the loaf for 20 minutes. Reduce the oven's temperature to 375°F (191°C), remove the Dutch oven's lid and bake the bread for 35 minutes. Reduce the oven's temperature again to 350°F (177°C) and bake the bread for 10 minutes, or until it is crispy and golden brown.

Place the hot sourdough on a wire rack to cool for 20 minutes before serving it warm. Wrap the completely cooled bread in a tea towel or beeswax wraps and store it in the fridge for up to 1 week.

Lemon Challah

When you eat a slice of this rich braided loaf, you will be amazed at how soft and light it is. This bread offers a sweet flavor that is enhanced by a burst of lemon. It is hard to believe that this gorgeous loaf is gluten-free! Citrus and sourdough pair together very well, and although this is still a bread, it is almost cakelike.

This bread can be baked in a loaf pan to give it a structured shape while still showing off the beautiful braided top, or it can be baked on a pizza stone to give it a slightly more rustic look. Either way, you will be creating a stunning and tasty bread!

Makes 1 loaf

Levain

30 g active starter

60 g warm water

30 g buckwheat flour

30 g brown rice flour

Loaf

40 g sweet white rice flour

65 g sorghum flour

40 g buckwheat flour

50 g brown rice flour

70 g tapioca starch

20 g brown sugar

5 g salt

120 g warm water

20 g olive oil

55 g milk, at room temperature

2 large eggs, at room temperature

23 g whole psyllium husk

4 g flaxseed, finely ground

½ tsp lemon zest

1 tsp fresh lemon juice

White rice flour, as needed

1 tbsp (9 g) sesame seeds

Reactivate your starter the day before you plan on building the levain. A good time to do this is when you get up in the morning, to allow the starter 6 to 8 hours to become bubbly and active. You will need 30 grams for the levain and at least 20 grams left over for maintaining your original starter/main culture (see page 14 for more information on the feeding ratio).

Build the levain: Using a kitchen scale, weigh 30 grams of active starter in a clean 500-milliliter jar. Vigorously whisk in 60 grams of warm water, then add 30 grams of buckwheat flour and 30 grams of brown rice flour. Ferment the levain for 6 to 8 hours, or until it is bubbly and has risen to a peak, before mixing it into the dough.

Mix the dough: In a large bowl, combine the sweet white rice flour, sorghum flour, buckwheat flour, brown rice flour, tapioca starch, brown sugar and salt. In a medium bowl, combine the warm water, olive oil and milk. Beat in the eggs. Stir the psyllium husk and flaxseed. Immediately whisk this mixture to prevent lumps from forming, then mix in the levain, lemon zest and lemon juice. Pour the lemon mixture into the flour blend. Combine the ingredients well with a kitchen mixer fitted with a dough hook running at medium-low speed, until all the ingredients are fully incorporated. You can also mix this dough with your hands, but it is quite sticky and soft.

Ferment: Form the dough into a ball, then place it in a 4-cup (1-L) proofing bowl. Cover the bowl with its lid and place it in the oven with the light on. Let the dough rest for 30 to 60 minutes, or until the dough begins to rise a little. Place the covered bowl in the fridge overnight for the bulk fermentation.

(continued)

Lemon Challah (continued)

Glaze

1 tsp olive oil

10 g fresh lemon juice

10 g granulated sugar

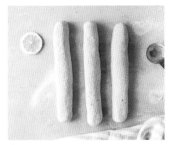

Shape the dough into 3 logs.

Attach the 3 logs at the top and braid them.

Braid the strands and tuck each end underneath.

Shape: The next day, remove the dough from the fridge and leave it at room temperature for 30 minutes, until it is warm enough to work with. Lightly dampen a work surface with water. Place a large piece of parchment paper next to the prepared work surface. Transfer the dough to the prepared work surface. Knead the dough with wet hands for 2 to 3 minutes. With a bench scraper, divide the dough into three equal portions weighing 252 grams each and shape them into logs. Dust the logs with a little white rice flour. With the palm of your hands, roll the three logs until they are 9 inches (23 cm) long. Place the dough strands on the parchment paper and braid them together just like you would braid hair: Attach and pinch together the three dough logs at one end, then take the left log and place it over the middle log. Take the right log and place it over the new middle log and repeat this process to the end of the dough strands. (See the photos for braiding details.) Pinch the ends closed and tuck each end underneath the braid. Place the braided dough, still on the parchment paper, in a 11 x 5 x 5–inch (28 x 13 x 13–cm) loaf pan to support the sides of the dough as it rises to create a structured look to the bread. If you prefer a rustic look, leave the dough on the parchment paper.

Proof: Cover the dough with a damp tea towel and let it rest at room temperature—ideally about 72°F (22°C)—for 3 to 5 hours. The proofing time depends on the temperature of your kitchen. If the temperature is a little colder, place the dough in the oven with the light on. In the summer warmth, it can be left on the counter, and it may benefit from less proofing time. When the dough has proofed enough, it will have risen and will feel soft, puffy and spongy on top. Chill the dough in the refrigerator for about 40 minutes before baking it, as this is necessary for the loaf to hold its shape. When ready to bake, sprinkle the sesame seeds on top of the loaf.

To bake in a Dutch oven for the rustic-looking bread: Preheat the oven to 450°F (232°C) with a Dutch oven on the center rack. Bake the bread for 20 minutes. Remove the Dutch oven lid and reduce the oven's temperature to 375°F (191°C). Bake the bread for 25 minutes, until it is golden brown.

To bake in a loaf pan: Preheat the oven to 450°F (232°C) and place the pan on the center rack of the oven. Cover the loaf pan with its lid or use tented aluminum foil. Bake the bread for 20 minutes. Remove the loaf pan's lid and reduce the oven's temperature to 375°F (191°C). Bake the bread for 25 minutes, until it is golden brown.

Remove the loaf from the pan and transfer it to a wire rack to cool for 30 minutes before you slice it.

Make the glaze: While the oven is preheating, make the glaze. In a small bowl, combine the olive oil, lemon juice and granulated sugar. Brush half of the glaze on top of the dough and save the remaining glaze for the baked bread as soon as it comes out of the oven.

This bread is best served the day it is made, but you can store it, wrapped in a tea towel or beeswax wraps, on the counter for 1 to 2 days. Slice and freeze any remaining bread.

Chocolate *and* Hazelnut Babka

This babka is one of my family's favorites. It's a miraculous gluten-free sourdough baked to create a soft swirled dough with scrumptious, not-too-sweet layers of chocolate and hazelnuts. The mouthwatering smell and gooey chocolate goodness are addicting—I find it hard to walk by this bread without stealing a slice.

Makes 1 loaf

Levain

26 g active starter

52 g warm water

26 g buckwheat flour

26 g brown rice flour

Babka

40 g oat flour

80 g boiling water

75 g sorghum flour

50 g buckwheat flour

50 g brown rice flour

50 g millet flour

70 g tapioca starch

40 g brown sugar

7 g salt

1 large egg, at room temperature

15 g olive oil

220 g warm water

20 g whole psyllium husk

5 g flaxseed, finely ground

White rice flour, as needed

Reactivate your starter the day before you plan on building the levain. A good time to do this is when you get up in the morning, to allow the starter 6 to 8 hours to become bubbly and active. You will need 26 grams for the levain and at least 20 grams left over for maintaining your original starter/main culture (see page 14 for more information on the feeding ratio).

Build the levain: Using a kitchen scale, weigh 26 grams of active starter in a clean 500-milliliter jar. Vigorously mix in 52 grams of warm water, then add 26 grams of buckwheat flour and 26 grams of brown rice flour. Ferment the levain for 6 to 8 hours, or until it is bubbly and has risen to a peak, before mixing it into the dough.

Mix the dough: In a heatproof medium bowl, combine the oat flour and boiling water. Immediately stir this mixture to make a smooth paste. Set the oat paste aside to cool until it's lukewarm. Meanwhile, in a large bowl, combine the sorghum flour, buckwheat flour, brown rice flour, millet flour, tapioca starch, brown sugar and salt. Set the flour blend aside. When the oat paste has cooled, beat in the egg, olive oil and warm water. Stir the levain, psyllium husk and flaxseed into the liquids. Immediately whisk the mixture to prevent lumps from forming. Add the psyllium mixture to the flour blend. Mix the dough well by hand, or with a kitchen mixer fitted with a dough hook running at medium-low speed, until all the ingredients are fully incorporated.

Ferment: Form the dough into a ball, then place it in a 4-cup (1-L) proofing bowl. Cover the bowl with its lid and place it in the oven with the light on. Let the dough rest for 30 to 60 minutes, or until the dough begins to rise a little. Place the covered bowl in the fridge overnight for the bulk fermentation.

Shape and fill: Cut some parchment paper to fit an 11 x 5 x 5–inch (28 x 13 x 13–cm) loaf pan that has a lid, leaving extra paper hanging over the sides to make it easier to lower the dough into the pan. Remove the dough from the fridge and leave it at room temperature for 30 minutes.

(continued)

Chocolate *and* Hazelnut Babka (continued)

Filling

80 g roughly chopped hazelnuts

40 g brown sugar

80 g roughly chopped semisweet chocolate

20 g unsweetened cocoa powder

12 g cold butter

25 g water, at room temperature

Roll the dough into a log.

Cut the log in half and make an X with the two pieces.

Cross the two halves over again, below the X and at the top.

Meanwhile, prepare the filling. In a small skillet over medium-low heat, toast the hazelnuts for 5 minutes, stirring them frequently to prevent them from burning, until they are slightly browned. In a medium saucepan over medium-low heat, combine the brown sugar, chocolate, cocoa powder, butter and water. Warm the ingredients for about 5 minutes, stirring them constantly, until the chocolate and butter are melted and the mixture becomes a spreadable paste. You may need to add a few extra drops of water if the mixture is too thick. Pour some hot water into a cup and place a metal spatula or butter knife in the water—the warmth of the spatula will help you spread the chocolate as it cools and becomes harder to spread. Fill a large heatproof bowl with hot water, then place a smaller heatproof bowl next to it. Transfer the melted chocolate mixture to the smaller bowl. Place the smaller bowl inside the larger bowl to keep the chocolate mixture warm and spreadable.

Lightly dust a work surface with the white rice flour. Transfer the dough to the prepared work surface. Knead the dough for 2 to 3 minutes, until it is well combined and smooth. Roll the dough out into a 10 x 12–inch (25 x 30–cm) rectangle that is ¼ inch (6 mm) thick. Spread the chocolate mixture over the dough's entire surface, and then evenly spread the hazelnuts on top of the chocolate. Roll the dough into a log, making sure to keep the first few rolls tight without straining and tearing the dough. Cut the log in half lengthwise and gently turn the halves so the filling is facing up. Twist the two halves together by making an X in the center and then crossing the two halves over each other between the center and the ends. (See the photos for shaping details.) Pinch and evenly round out the ends, and then place the dough on the parchment paper. Lower the parchment paper with the dough into the loaf pan.

Proof: Place the dough, still in the loaf pan, inside a reusable plastic bag and let it rest at room temperature—ideally about 72°F (22°C)—for 3 to 5 hours. The proofing time depends on the temperature of your kitchen. If the temperature is a little colder, place the dough in the oven with the light on. In the summer warmth, it can be left on the counter, and it may benefit from less proofing time. When the dough has proofed enough, it will have risen and will feel soft, puffy and spongy on top.

Bake: Preheat the oven to 400°F (204°C). While the oven is preheating, chill the dough in the refrigerator. Then, remove the dough from the fridge and cover the loaf pan with its lid or a tented piece of aluminum foil. Bake the bread on the oven's middle rack for 25 minutes. Reduce the oven's temperature to 350°F (177°C), remove the loaf pan's lid and bake the bread for 25 to 30 minutes. The bread will rise and become golden brown on top. It is done when a toothpick inserted into the center comes out clean.

Set the loaf pan on a wire rack, and let the loaf cool for 30 minutes before removing it from the pan.

This bread tastes the best the day it is made, but you can store it, covered in a tea towel or beeswax wrap, on the counter for 2 to 3 days. After 2 to 3 days, store the bread in the fridge, keeping it covered, for up to 1 week.

Sticky Cinnamon Buns

These cinnamon buns are sweet and incredibly delicious—you will soon be reaching for another one! I always share these buns, because otherwise I would eat them all. Mixing the dough and baking the buns is almost as fun as eating them, thanks to the heavenly aroma of the cinnamon.

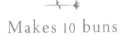

Makes 10 buns

Levain

40 g active starter

80 g warm water

40 g buckwheat flour

40 g brown rice flour

Buns

70 g sorghum flour

50 g buckwheat flour

50 g sweet white rice flour

50 g oat flour

30 g brown sugar

7 g salt

60 g warm water

150 g milk, at room temperature

1 large egg, at room temperature

21 g whole psyllium husk

8 g flaxseed, finely ground

White rice flour, as needed

Reactivate your starter the day before you plan on building the levain. A good time to do this is when you get up in the morning, to allow the starter 6 to 8 hours to become bubbly and active. You will need 40 grams for the levain and at least 20 grams left over for maintaining your original starter/main culture (see page 14 for more information on the feeding ratio).

Build the levain: Using a kitchen scale, weigh 40 grams of starter in a clean 500-milliliter jar. Vigorously mix in 80 grams of warm water, then add 40 grams of buckwheat flour and 40 grams of brown rice flour. Ferment the levain for 6 to 8 hours, or until it is bubbly and has risen to a peak, before mixing it into the dough.

Mix the dough: In a large bowl, combine the sorghum flour, buckwheat flour, sweet white rice flour, oat flour, brown sugar and salt. In a medium bowl, combine the warm water and milk, and then beat in the egg. Stir the psyllium husk and flaxseed. Immediately whisk this mixture to prevent lumps from forming. Add the levain to the psyllium mixture, then pour the levain-psyllium mixture into the flour blend. Mix the dough well by hand, or with a kitchen mixer fitted with a dough hook running at medium-low speed, until all the ingredients are fully incorporated.

Ferment: Form the dough into a ball, then place it in a 4-cup (1-L) proofing bowl. Cover the bowl with its lid and place it in the oven with the light on. Let the dough rest for 30 to 60 minutes, or until the dough begins to rise a little. Place the covered bowl in the fridge overnight for the bulk fermentation.

Shape: The next day, remove the dough from the fridge and leave it at room temperature for 30 minutes, until it is warm enough to work with.

(continued)

Sticky Cinnamon Buns (continued)

Filling

100 g raisins

30 g water, at room temperature

80 g softened butter

6 g ground cinnamon

110 g brown sugar

Glaze

60 g cream cheese, at room temperature

80 g powdered sugar

25 g milk, at room temperature

Meanwhile, begin preparing the filling. In a small saucepan over medium heat, combine the raisins and water. Warm the ingredients until the water almost boils, then turn off the heat. Cover the saucepan and allow the raisins to soak while you knead and shape the dough.

Lightly dust a work surface with the white rice flour. Place a large rectangular piece of plastic wrap next to the prepared work surface. Finally, line a medium pizza stone or baking sheet with parchment paper. Transfer the dough to the prepared work surface. Knead the dough for 2 to 3 minutes, and then place the dough on the plastic wrap. With a rolling pin, roll the dough until it measures 15 x 11 inches (38 x 28 cm). Begin filling the dough by using a spatula to smear the softened butter across the dough's entire surface. Sprinkle the cinnamon and brown sugar on top of the butter. Drain any excess water from the raisins, then sprinkle them over the cinnamon sugar. Working from the longest side of the dough, gently roll the dough into a log, keeping the plastic wrap on the outside to prevent tearing the dough. Flatten both ends of the log by patting them toward the center of the log with your hands. Slice the log into ten equal pieces. Place the dough pieces on the prepared pizza stone.

Proof: Cover the dough with a damp tea towel and let it rest at room temperature—ideally about 72°F (22°C)—for 3 to 5 hours. The proofing time depends on the temperature of your kitchen. If the temperature is a little colder, place the dough in the oven with the light on. In the summer warmth, it can be left on the counter, and it may benefit from less proofing time. When the dough has proofed enough, it will have risen and will feel soft, puffy and spongy on top.

Bake: Preheat the oven to 425°F (218°C). Bake the buns, still on the pizza stone, on the oven's middle rack for 15 minutes. Reduce the oven's temperature to 350°F (177°C) and bake the buns for 15 minutes, or until they are light golden brown and the filling is bubbly and brown.

While the buns are baking, prepare the glaze. In a medium bowl, beat together the cream cheese and powdered sugar with a handheld mixer. Slowly add the milk and beat the mixture again until the glaze is smooth and is at a consistency you like.

Let the buns cool for 5 minutes, then use a spatula to spread the glaze over the buns. Let the buns cool for another 20 minutes before removing them from the pizza stone.

These buns taste the best the day they are made, but they will last in an airtight container on the counter for up to 2 days. Any leftover buns can be frozen for up to 3 months.

Bacon *and* Onion Wheel

Robust flavors combine with the visual appeal of this savory pull-apart bread. This is an ideal snack or appetizer to enjoy with your family and friends. The preparation of this gluten-free dough may sound intimidating, but it is quite easy to shape. The satisfaction that comes with gazing at your masterpiece—and then eating it—is well worth giving this recipe a try.

To make this recipe quicker to prepare, it is convenient to cook the bacon and onion the night before you bake it. Leave the cooked bacon and onion in the fridge for the night to give the mixture ample time to cool.

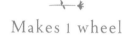

Makes 1 wheel

Levain

40 g active starter
80 g warm water
40 g buckwheat flour
40 g brown rice flour

Wheel

40 g millet flour
70 g tapioca starch
75 g sorghum flour
40 g oat flour
20 g quinoa flour
15 g teff flour
5 g salt
220 g warm water
100 g warm milk
15 g pure maple syrup
24 g whole psyllium husk
4 g flaxseed, finely ground
White rice flour, as needed

Reactivate your starter the day before you plan on building the levain. A good time to do this is when you get up in the morning, to allow the starter 6 to 8 hours to become bubbly and active. You will need 40 grams for the levain and at least 20 grams left over for maintaining your original starter/main culture (see page 14 for more information on the feeding ratio).

Build the levain: Using a kitchen scale, weigh 40 grams of active starter in a clean 500-milliliter jar. Vigorously mix in 80 grams of warm water, then add 40 grams of buckwheat flour and 40 grams of brown rice flour. Ferment the levain for 6 to 8 hours, or until it is bubbly and has risen to a peak, before mixing it into the dough.

Mix the dough: In a large bowl, combine the millet flour, tapioca starch, sorghum flour, oat flour, quinoa flour, teff flour and salt. In a medium bowl, combine the warm water, warm milk, maple syrup and levain. Sprinkle the psyllium husk and flaxseed on top of the levain mixture. Immediately whisk the ingredients to prevent lumps from forming. Pour the levain-psyllium mixture into the flour blend. Mix the dough well by hand, or with a kitchen mixer fitted with a dough hook running at medium-low speed, until all the ingredients are fully incorporated.

Ferment: Form the dough into a ball, then place it in a 4-cup (1-L) proofing bowl. Cover the bowl with its lid and place it in the oven with the light on. Let the dough rest for 30 to 60 minutes, or until the dough begins to rise a little. Place the covered bowl in the fridge overnight for the bulk fermentation.

(continued)

Bacon *and* Onion Wheel (continued)

Filling

130 g diced bacon (3 strips)

200 g diced onion (1 large onion)

½ tsp salt

⅛ tsp black pepper

80 g sour cream

Shape: The next day, remove the dough from the fridge and leave it at room temperature for about 30 minutes, until it is warm enough to work with. Meanwhile, cut two 10½-inch (26-cm)-diameter circles of parchment paper. Set the parchment paper aside. In a medium skillet over medium-low heat, combine the bacon and onion. Cook the mixture for 6 to 8 minutes, until the bacon is crispy and the onion is translucent. Drain and discard the excess fat from the bacon and onion mixture, and then leave the bacon and onion to cool while you shape the dough.

Lightly dampen a work surface with water. Transfer the dough to the prepared work surface. Knead the dough with wet hands to form it into a ball. Lightly dust the dough's surface with the white rice flour, and then knead the dough for 1 to 2 minutes, until it is smooth and holding together well. Cut the dough in half. Weigh each half to ensure each one is 398 grams. Shape each piece of dough into a ball. Place a dough ball on each of the parchment paper circles. Flatten each ball with your hand, and then roll it out into two 10-inch (25-cm) round disks.

Mix the salt and pepper into the sour cream, spread the sour cream on top of one dough disk, then evenly spread the bacon and onion mixture on top of the sour cream. Carefully flip the second dough disk directly on top of the filling and peel off the parchment paper. Gently smooth the top layer of dough with your hands. Seal the outer edges together by pinching them with your fingers. Place a small glass—such as a shot glass—in the center of the dough circle to make a ring indentation, being careful not to cut all the way through the dough. Cut the dough into even quarters, being careful not to cut into the center ring. Cut each quarter segment in half to make eight segments, again being careful not to cut all the way to the center. Then, cut each of the eight segments in half to make sixteen segments, again being careful not to cut all the way to the center. Gently twist each segment three times to form 16 twisted bread sticks that are still attached to the center. Remove the shot glass and score several lines to form a star shape in the center circle. Transfer the dough, still on the parchment paper, to a large pizza stone.

Evenly spread the sour cream, bacon and onion over the dough.

Top the filling with the dough disk, add the shot glass and cut into eight even pieces.

Cut the eight pieces in half and twist.

Remove the shot glass before baking.

Glaze

10 g soy sauce, at room temperature

10 g pure maple syrup, at room temperature

10 g water, at room temperature

Proof: Cover the dough with a damp tea towel and let it rest at room temperature—ideally about 72°F (22°C)—for 2 to 3 hours. The proofing time depends on the temperature of your kitchen. If the temperature is a little colder, place the dough in the oven with the light on. In the summer warmth, it can be left on the counter, and it may benefit from less proofing time. When the dough has proofed enough, it will have risen and will feel soft, puffy and spongy on top.

Bake: Preheat the oven to 450°F (232°C). In the meantime, prepare the glaze. In a small bowl, whisk together the soy sauce, maple syrup and water. Set the glaze aside. Bake the wheel on the pizza stone for 15 minutes. Reduce the oven's temperature to 375°F (191°C) and bake the wheel for 20 minutes. Remove the wheel from the oven and brush the glaze on top. Bake the glazed wheel for 10 minutes, until it is golden brown and a toothpick inserted into the center comes out clean. If you like the wheel a little crispier, you can bake it for an extra 10 minutes at 350°F (177°C).

Serve the wheel warm from the oven. Cover any leftovers with beeswax wraps and place them in the fridge. You can also reheat the wheel the following day in a 350°F (177°C) oven for 10 minutes.

quick ❧ ❧ breads, *sourdough-* style

These loaves are not your store-bought loaf of gluten-free bread. They come from the sweeter side of sourdough! I love the fact that sourdough can be modified to suit a sweeter bread like the Blueberry and Apple Muffins (page 132) or made tangier for the savory side like my Southern Sourdough Cornbread (page 129).

An easy way to handle gluten-free sourdough is to mix up a batter; add some fruit, nuts, seeds and spices; and drop the dough in a loaf pan to rise—let the fermentation do all the work! The Swirled Cinnamon and Raisin Bread (page 123) is one of my favorite loaf pan breads and a close competitor with the Overnight Banana Bread (page 126), which is by far the softest and tastiest gluten-free banana bread I have ever eaten.

Typically, quick breads are breads that require very little preparation time. The assembly of the gluten-free breads in this chapter is not time-consuming, but some of the recipes require a longer overnight fermentation due to the addition of sourdough—don't worry, the final product is more than worth it!

Seed *and* Fig Loaf

Mix together some whole grains, banana, figs and seeds and soon you will be eating a most delicious bread. There are so many healthy foods packed into this one loaf with just the right amount of sweetness. I chose to include this recipe in the cookbook because it reminds me of fruit and nut snack bars, but on the softer, cakelike side. Letting this loaf rise and ferment brings out the tastiest flavors and the best texture, with an amazing natural sweetness from the dried fruit.

Makes 1 loaf

Levain

30 g active starter

60 g warm water

30 g buckwheat flour

30 g brown rice flour

Loaf

20 g boiling water

30 g buckwheat groats

60 g buckwheat flour

40 g oat flour

40 g millet flour

30 g teff flour

30 g whole oats

30 g brown sugar

6 g salt

20 g hemp seeds

50 g roughly chopped raw unsalted sunflower seeds

15 g chia seeds

½ tsp ground cinnamon

1 tsp unsweetened cocoa powder

Reactivate your starter the day before you plan on building the levain. A good time to do this is when you get up in the morning, to allow the starter 6 to 8 hours to become bubbly and active. You will need 30 grams for the levain and at least 20 grams for maintaining your original starter/main culture (see page 14 for more information on the feeding ratio).

Build the levain: Using a kitchen scale, weigh 30 grams of active starter in a clean 500-milliliter jar. Vigorously whisk in 60 grams of warm water, then add 30 grams of buckwheat flour and 30 grams of brown rice flour. Ferment the levain for 6 to 8 hours, or until it is bubbly and has risen to a peak, before mixing it into the dough.

Mix the dough: Line an 8 x 5 x 4–inch (20 x 13 x 10–cm) loaf pan with parchment paper. In a small heatproof dish, pour the boiling water over the buckwheat groats and let them soak while you prepare the rest of the dough. In a large bowl, combine the buckwheat flour, oat flour, millet flour, teff flour, oats, brown sugar, salt, hemp seeds, chopped sunflower seeds, chia seeds, cinnamon and cocoa powder. In a medium bowl, combine the room-temperature water, olive oil and molasses. Stir in the psyllium husk. Whisk the mixture immediately to prevent lumps from forming, then mix in the levain, soaked buckwheat groats, banana and figs. Add the seed and fig mixture to the flour blend. Mix the dough well by hand, or with a kitchen mixer fitted with a dough hook running at medium-low speed, until all the ingredients are fully incorporated. The dough will have the consistency of porridge.

Ferment: Transfer the dough to the prepared loaf pan. Cover the loaf pan with plastic wrap and let the dough rest in a warm location for 30 to 60 minutes, until the dough just begins to rise. Place the covered loaf pan in the fridge overnight for the bulk fermentation. Alternatively, you can leave the dough to rise for 3 to 4 hours in a warm place and then bake it.

(continued)

Loaf (cont.)

270 g water, at room temperature

15 g olive oil

15 g molasses, at room temperature

18 g whole psyllium husk

80 g mashed banana (1 medium banana)

30 g finely chopped figs or raisins

White rice flour, as needed

Whole raw unsalted sunflower seeds, as needed

Proof: The next day, remove the dough from the fridge and leave it, still covered, at room temperature—ideally about 72°F (22°C)—for 3 to 5 hours. The proofing time depends on the temperature of your kitchen. If the temperature is a little colder, place the dough in the oven with the light on. In the summer warmth, it can be left on the counter, and it may benefit from less proofing time. When the dough has proofed enough, it will have risen and will feel soft, puffy and spongy on top.

Score: Preheat the oven to 350°F (177°C). Lightly dampen the dough with water and dust some white rice flour on the top. Lightly score a tree trunk on the top of the dough and place the whole sunflower seeds around the design to make leaves.

Bake: Bake the loaf for 45 minutes, or until it feels firm to the touch and a toothpick inserted into the center comes out clean.

Let the loaf cool in the pan on a wire rack for 10 minutes. Remove the loaf from the pan and allow it to cool for 30 minutes before slicing it.

Store this loaf, covered, on the counter for up to 2 days. Slice and freeze the remainder. This bread will keep in the freezer for up to 3 months.

Swirled Cinnamon *and* Raisin Bread

Whenever I smell raisin bread toasting, I always crave it. I just had to include a recipe for cinnamon and raisin bread in this cookbook! This gluten-free recipe allows you to indulge your cinnamon and raisin cravings in a celiac-friendly way. It never lasts more than a few days at my house.

Plumping the raisins by soaking them makes all the difference to the baked loaf.

Makes 1 loaf

Levain
30 g active starter
60 g warm water
30 g buckwheat flour
30 g brown rice flour

Raisins
50 g raisins
30 g warm water

Loaf
70 g white rice flour
60 g tapioca starch
50 g sorghum flour
50 g oat flour
20 g buckwheat flour
7 g salt
190 g warm water
60 g warm milk
20 g honey
1 large egg, at room temperature
18 g whole psyllium husk
4 g flaxseed, finely ground

Reactivate your starter the day before you plan on building the levain. A good time to do this is when you get up in the morning, to allow the starter 6 to 8 hours to become bubbly and active. You will need 30 grams for the levain and at least 20 grams for maintaining your original starter/main culture (see page 14 for more information on the feeding ratio).

Build the levain: Using a kitchen scale, weigh 30 grams of active starter in a clean 500-milliliter jar. Vigorously mix in 60 grams of warm water, then add 30 grams of buckwheat flour and 30 grams of brown rice flour. Ferment the levain for 6 to 8 hours, or until it is bubbly and has risen to a peak, before mixing it into the dough.

Soak the raisins and mix the dough: In a small bowl, soak the raisins in the warm water for 1 to 2 hours prior to mixing the dough, then drain any remaining water. To begin preparing the loaf, combine the white rice flour, tapioca starch, sorghum flour, oat flour, buckwheat flour and salt in a large bowl. In a medium bowl, combine the warm water, warm milk and honey. Beat in the egg and levain. Stir the psyllium husk and flaxseed into the mixture, and whisk the mixture immediately to prevent lumps from forming. Add the levain mixture to the flour blend. Mix the dough well by hand, or with a kitchen mixer fitted with a dough hook running at medium-low speed, until all the ingredients are fully incorporated. Fold in the raisins.

Ferment: Form the dough into a ball, then place it in a 4-cup (1-L) proofing bowl. Cover the bowl with its lid and place it in the oven with the light on. Let the dough rest for 30 to 60 minutes, or until the dough begins to rise a little. Place the covered bowl in the fridge overnight for the bulk fermentation.

(continued)

Swirled Cinnamon *and* Raisin Bread (continued)

Filling

30 g melted butter

60 g brown sugar, divided

3 g ground cinnamon, divided

Shape: The next day, remove the dough from the fridge and leave it at room temperature for about 30 minutes, until it is warm enough to work with. Line a 9 x 5–inch (23 x 13–cm) loaf pan with parchment paper. Lightly dampen a work surface with water. Transfer the dough to the prepared work surface. Knead the dough with wet hands for 2 to 3 minutes, until it is somewhat smooth. Roll out the dough into a 9 x 7–inch (23 x 18–cm) rectangle. To prepare the filling, brush the melted butter over the dough's surface. Sprinkle two-thirds of the brown sugar and two-thirds of the cinnamon on top of the butter. Pick up one of the short sides of the dough and fold it a quarter of the way over the rest of the dough. Spread half of the remaining brown sugar and cinnamon on the top of the fold. Fold the dough over again and spread the remaining brown sugar and cinnamon on the top. Roll the dough to the end and shape it to fit the loaf pan. This will create a swirled effect. This is a wet, sticky dough that will tear easily, but because it will be baked in a loaf pan, you can easily pinch and seal any holes. Poke the raisins that are sticking out of the dough back in to prevent them from burning. Smooth the dough over the holes created by the raisins.

Proof: Cover the dough with a damp tea towel and let it rest at room temperature—ideally about 72°F (22°C)—for 2 to 3 hours. The proofing time depends on the temperature of your kitchen. If the temperature is a little colder, place the dough in the oven with the light on. In the summer warmth, it can be left on the counter, and it may benefit from less proofing time. When the dough has proofed enough, it will have risen and will feel soft, puffy and spongy on top.

Bake: Preheat the oven to 450°F (232°C). Bake the loaf for 15 minutes. Reduce the oven's temperature to 375°F (191°C) and bake the loaf for 25 to 30 minutes, until it feels firm on top and a toothpick inserted into the center comes out clean.

Let the loaf cool for 30 minutes, then remove it from the pan and slice it.

Wrap the bread in a tea towel or beeswax wraps and store it on the counter for up to 2 days. This bread can be frozen for up to 3 months.

 Overnight Banana Bread

You would never guess this banana bread is gluten-free, because it is so light and fluffy. This recipe was developed during the time we were forced to stay home during the COVID-19 pandemic, and the bread soon became a family favorite. Even people who do not need to eat a gluten-free diet have raved about this one. The sourdough and the overnight fermentation bring out exceptional texture and enhanced flavor. The coffee icing is a nod to the way my mum always made her banana bread.

If you are using frozen bananas, you will need to drain some of the extra liquid that comes from freezing; otherwise, that liquid can create a thin, soupy batter and a wet dough that takes longer to bake.

Makes 1 loaf

Levain

30 g active starter
60 g warm water
30 g buckwheat flour
30 g brown rice flour

Loaf

50 g almond flour
55 g oat flour
60 g tapioca flour
1 tsp baking soda
3 g unsweetened cocoa powder
1 tsp salt
50 g butter, at room temperature
170 g brown sugar
2 large eggs, at room temperature
15 g honey
350 g mashed ripe bananas (about 3 medium bananas)
10 g whole psyllium husk

Reactivate your starter the day before you plan on building the levain. A good time to do this is when you get up in the morning, to allow the starter 6 to 8 hours to become bubbly and active. You will need 30 grams for the levain and at least 20 grams for maintaining your original starter/main culture (see page 14 for more information on the feeding ratio).

Build the levain: Using a kitchen scale, weigh 30 grams of active starter in a clean 500-milliliter jar. Vigorously whisk in 60 grams of warm water, then add 30 grams of buckwheat flour and 30 grams of brown rice flour. Ferment the levain for 6 to 8 hours, or until it is bubbly and has risen to a peak, before mixing it into the dough.

Mix the dough: Line a 8 x 5 x 4–inch (20 x 13 x 10–cm) loaf pan with parchment paper. In a large bowl, combine the almond flour, oat flour, tapioca starch, baking soda, cocoa powder and salt. In a medium bowl, use a handheld mixer to beat together the butter and brown sugar for about 2 minutes, until they are smooth and creamy. Add the eggs, honey and bananas and beat the ingredients together until they are well combined. Add the levain to the butter mixture, then sprinkle the psyllium husk on top of the mixture. Immediately beat everything together to combine the ingredients and prevent lumps from forming. Add the levain-psyllium mixture to the flour blend. Mix the dough well with a spoon, or with a kitchen mixer fitted with a dough hook running at medium-low speed, until all the ingredients are fully incorporated. The dough will have the consistency of cake batter. Pour the dough into the prepared loaf pan, then cover the pan with plastic wrap.

(continued)

Coffee Icing

15 g softened butter

15 g strongly brewed warm coffee

150 g powdered sugar

Proof: Let the dough rest at room temperature—ideally about 72°F (22°C)—for 7 to 9 hours. The proofing time depends on the temperature of your kitchen. If the temperature is a little colder, place the dough in the oven with the light on. In the summer warmth, it can be left on the counter, and it may benefit from less proofing time. When the dough has proofed enough, it will have risen to nearly the top of the loaf pan and will be soft and spongy.

For the icing: Add the butter to a medium bowl and pour in the warm coffee. Gently stir or beat in the powdered sugar, until it is a smooth and easily spreadable consistency. You may need to add a little more powdered sugar or coffee to reach the desired consistency.

Bake: Preheat the oven to 350°F (177°C). Bake the loaf for 1 hour, or until it feels set on the top and a toothpick inserted into the center comes out clean.

Let the bread cool completely in the pan before removing it and spreading the icing on the top.

Store the bread, tightly wrapped in a tea towel or beeswax wraps, on the counter for 2 days. Slice and freeze any that is left over after that time.

Southern *Sourdough* Cornbread

This is a gluten-free sourdough version of a traditional cornbread that is simple to mix up and loaded with flavor. Cornmeal can be purchased in coarse to finely ground consistencies, and the texture you use will affect the amount of water the cornmeal soaks up. A coarser cornmeal will not absorb as much water as more finely ground cornmeal. For this recipe, I use finely ground cornmeal, so make sure you choose finely ground as well.

I adore the combined flavors of jalapeños and cheese, which take this cornbread to a whole new level. I have made this recipe with and without the addition of jalapeños and cheese, but I definitely prefer the hot, cheesy flavor combination.

Makes 1 loaf

Levain

40 g active starter

80 g warm water

40 g buckwheat flour

40 g brown rice flour

Loaf

160 g finely ground cornmeal

280 g milk, at room temperature

60 g tapioca starch

50 g sweet white rice flour

40 g sorghum flour

50 g oat flour

8 g salt

1 tsp ground mustard

40 g butter, at room temperature

50 g granulated sugar

3 large eggs, at room temperature

30 g mayonnaise, at room temperature

5 g whole psyllium husk

5 g flaxseed, finely ground

1 to 2 medium jalapeños, diced (optional)

100 g grated Cheddar cheese (optional)

Reactivate your starter the day before you plan on building the levain. A good time to do this is when you get up in the morning, to allow the starter 6 to 8 hours to become bubbly and active. You will need 40 grams for the levain and at least 20 grams for maintaining your original starter/main culture (see page 14 for more information on the feeding ratio).

Build the levain: Using a kitchen scale, weigh 40 grams of active starter in a clean 500-milliliter jar. Vigorously whisk in 80 grams of warm water, then add 40 grams of buckwheat flour and 40 grams of brown rice flour. Ferment the levain for 6 to 8 hours, or until it is bubby and has risen to a peak, before mixing it into the dough.

Mix the dough: Line a 11 x 5 x 5–inch (28 x 13 x 13–cm) pan with parchment paper. In a medium bowl, soak the cornmeal in the milk. Meanwhile, in a large bowl, combine the tapioca starch, sweet white rice flour, sorghum flour, oat flour, salt and ground mustard. In a medium bowl, use a handheld mixer to beat together the butter and sugar for about 2 minutes, until they are smooth and creamy. Then, beat in the eggs, mayonnaise, soaked cornmeal and levain. Sprinkle the psyllium husk and flaxseed on top of the levain mixture. Immediately beat the ingredients together to prevent lumps from forming. Add the levain-psyllium mixture to the flour blend. Add the jalapeños (if using) and Cheddar cheese (if using). Mix the dough well with a spoon, or with a kitchen mixer fitted with a dough hook running at medium-low speed, until all the ingredients are fully incorporated. The dough will have the consistency of cake batter. Transfer the dough to the prepared loaf pan and cover it with plastic wrap.

(continued)

Southern *Sourdough* Cornbread (continued)

Proof: Let the dough rest at room temperature—ideally about 72°F (22°C)—for 3 to 4 hours. The proofing time depends on the temperature of your kitchen. If the temperature is a little colder, place the dough in the oven with the light on. In the summer warmth, it can be left on the counter, and it may benefit from less proofing time. When the dough has proofed enough, it will have risen and feel soft and spongy on the top.

Bake: Preheat the oven to 400°F (204°C). Bake the cornbread for 15 minutes, then reduce the oven's temperature to 350°F (177°C) and bake the cornbread for 30 minutes, until the top is firm and set and a toothpick inserted into the center comes out clean.

Let the loaf cool in the pan for 20 minutes before removing it and placing it on a wire rack. Let it cool on the wire rack for 1 to 2 hours before slicing it.

Wrap the cornbread in a tea towel or beeswax wraps and store it on the counter for 1 to 2 days. If your cornbread begins to dry out too quickly, it is best to slice and freeze the remainder. The cornbread will last in the freezer for up to 3 months.

Blueberry *and* Apple Muffins

Everyone needs a great muffin recipe—and with all of the simple gluten-free ingredients in this recipe, these muffins are on the healthier side. Juicy blueberries and pureed apples add sweetness to these fluffy and delicious muffins. Use either frozen or fresh blueberries—both are equally good. You can also top these muffins with the optional icing for a fun treat. They make a wonderful afternoon pick-me-up accompanied with a cup of coffee or tea.

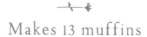

Makes 13 muffins

Levain

30 g active starter

60 g warm water

30 g buckwheat flour

30 g brown rice flour

Muffins

40 g oat flour

20 g almond flour

20 g sweet white rice flour

20 g tapioca starch

30 g sorghum flour

½ tsp ground cinnamon

¼ tsp ground ginger

¼ tsp salt

40 g melted butter, at room temperature

70 g brown sugar

3 large eggs, at room temperature

50 g milk, at room temperature

8 g flaxseed, finely ground

100 g cooked pureed Gala apple

120 g fresh or thawed frozen blueberries

Reactivate your starter the day before you plan on building the levain. A good time to do this is when you get up in the morning, to allow the starter 6 to 8 hours to become bubbly and active. You will need 30 grams for the levain and at least 20 grams for maintaining your original starter/main culture (see page 14 for more information on the feeding ratio).

Build the levain: Using a kitchen scale, weigh 30 grams of active starter in a clean 500-milliliter jar. Vigorously mix in 60 grams of warm water, then add 30 grams of buckwheat flour and 30 grams of brown rice flour. Ferment the levain for 6 to 8 hours, or until it is bubbly and has risen to a peak, before mixing it into the dough.

Mix the batter: If you would like standard-size muffins, line a standard 12-well muffin pan with paper baking liners. Line one well of a second standard muffin pan with a paper baking liner. In a large bowl, combine the oat flour, almond flour, sweet white rice flour, tapioca starch, sorghum flour, cinnamon, ginger and salt. In a medium bowl, use a handheld mixer to beat together the butter and brown sugar until combined. Then, beat in the eggs. Add the levain and milk to the butter mixture, and then stir in the flaxseed. Add the levain-flaxseed mixture to the flour blend, mixing everything together until there is no loose flour. Fold in the apple and blueberries. Spoon the batter into the prepared muffin pans, making sure each muffin well is just over three-fourths full. Cover the muffin pans with plastic wrap.

(continued)

Blueberry *and* Apple Muffins (continued)

Optional Icing

25 g cold butter, cubed

70 g powdered sugar

10 g fresh lemon juice

Proof: Let the batter rest at room temperature—ideally about 72°F (22°C)—for 2 to 3 hours. The proofing time depends on the temperature of your kitchen. If the temperature is a little colder, place the muffin pan in the oven with the light on. In the summer warmth, it can be left on the counter, and the batter may benefit from less proofing time. When the batter has proofed enough, it will have risen, will feel soft and spongy and will be slightly domed on top.

Bake: Preheat the oven to 350°F (177°C). Bake the muffins for 20 to 25 minutes, or until they are set on the top and a toothpick inserted into the center comes out clean.

Remove the muffins from the muffin pans and place them on a wire rack to cool for 15 minutes.

While the muffins are cooling, prepare the icing (if using). Melt the butter in a small saucepan over low heat. Turn off the heat, and then stir in the powdered sugar and lemon juice. Stir the icing until it is smooth. Spread the icing on the warm muffins.

Serve the muffins while they are warm. Leftovers can be stored, covered, on the counter for up to 2 days. After 2 days, freeze any remaining muffins.

Date *and* Orange Scones

Making and baking these scones is just about as amazing as eating them—the smell of fresh orange is so uplifting. When you first bite into these scones, you taste the orange with just a hint of dates. These beauties boast a soft center and a light, crispy outer crust that makes it hard to guess that they are gluten-free.

Scones in all forms are a favorite of mine, and they always remind me of my sister Susan. She makes the best date scones ever, and she's the most talented baker I know. But these gluten-free scones are pretty spectacular, if I do say so myself!

Makes 8 scones

Levain

25 g active starter

50 g warm water

25 g buckwheat flour

25 g brown rice flour

Scones

40 g oat flour

65 g brown rice flour

60 g sorghum flour

70 g tapioca starch

30 g granulated sugar

1 tsp baking powder

½ tsp salt

2 large eggs, at room temperature

70 g plain, unsweetened full-fat Greek yogurt, at room temperature

50 g milk, at room temperature

10 g whole psyllium husk

100 g grated cold butter

100 g gluten-free dates, roughly chopped

15 g finely grated orange zest

White rice flour, as needed

Reactivate your starter the day before you plan on building the levain. A good time to do this is when you get up in the morning, to allow the starter 6 to 8 hours to become bubbly and active. You will need 25 grams for the levain and at least 20 grams for maintaining your original starter/main culture (see page 14 for more information on the feeding ratio).

Build the levain: Using a kitchen scale, weigh 25 grams of active starter in a clean 500-milliliter jar. Vigorously mix in 50 grams of warm water, then add 25 grams of buckwheat flour and 25 grams of brown rice flour. Ferment the levain for 6 to 8 hours, or until it is bubbly and has risen to a peak, before mixing it into the dough.

Mix the dough: In a large bowl, combine the oat flour, brown rice flour, sorghum flour, tapioca starch, sugar, baking powder and salt. In a medium bowl, use a handheld mixer to beat together the eggs, Greek yogurt, milk and levain until the ingredients are aerated and evenly mixed. Sprinkle the psyllium husk on top of the levain mixture and beat the ingredients again, until they are just combined. Mix in the butter, dates and orange zest. Add the date-orange mixture to the flour blend. Mix the two together with a wooden spoon until all of the flour is incorporated and a dough forms.

Ferment: Place the dough in a 4-cup (1-L) proofing bowl. Cover the bowl with its lid and let the dough rest on the kitchen counter for about 2 hours, or until it begins to rise and feels soft and spongy on top.

Shape: Cut a piece of parchment paper to fit the bottom of your Dutch oven. Lightly dust a work surface with white rice flour. Transfer the dough to the prepared work surface. Knead it for 2 to 3 minutes, until it easily holds its shape. Shape the dough into a disk that is about 8 inches (20 cm) in diameter, and then place it on the parchment paper. Cut the dough into eight wedge-shaped pieces. Separate each piece by about 1 inch (2.5 cm).

(continued)

Date *and* Orange Scones (continued)

Optional Toppings

Butter or whipped cream and jam

Proof: Cover the dough with a damp tea towel or plastic wrap. Let the dough rest at room temperature—ideally about 72°F (22°C)—for 2 to 3 hours. The proofing time depends on the temperature of your kitchen. If the temperature is a little colder, place the dough in the oven with the light on. In the summer warmth, it can be left on the counter, and it may benefit from less proofing time. When the dough has proofed enough, it will have risen a little and feel slightly softer than it did before. Place the scones, still on the parchment paper, in the fridge to chill while the oven preheats.

Bake: If you will be baking the scones in a Dutch oven, preheat the oven to 425°F (218°C) with a Dutch oven on the middle rack. Remove the dough from the fridge and carefully slide the parchment paper and dough into the Dutch oven. Cover the Dutch oven with its lid and bake the scones for 15 minutes. Remove the Dutch oven's lid and bake the scones for 25 minutes, or until they are light brown on top and a toothpick inserted into the center comes out clean.

Place the hot scones on a wire rack to cool for 10 minutes. Serve them with the optional toppings of butter or whipped cream and jam.

Wrap the scones in a tea towel or beeswax wraps and store them on the counter for up to 2 days. The scones will keep in the freezer for up to 3 months.

Wholesome Carrot Cake

If you need to add more fruit and vegetables to your celiac diet, then this is the recipe to make. Once you realize how easy this sourdough carrot cake is, you will make it again and again. An overnight fermentation in the pan produces a delicious gluten-free cake loaded with carrots and apples. All you need to do when you wake up in the morning is turn on the oven, put the loaf in and then wait in anticipation. You must eat it with the cream cheese and yogurt icing!

—⊀—⊀

Makes 1 (9-inch [23-cm]) cake

Levain

25 g active starter

50 g warm water

25 g buckwheat flour

25 g brown rice flour

Cake

Olive oil, as needed

Sifted unsweetened cocoa powder, as needed

60 g almond flour

30 g sweet white rice flour

70 g oat flour

40 g buckwheat flour

60 g sorghum flour

75 g tapioca starch

1 tsp baking soda

7 g ground cinnamon

1 tsp ground ginger

½ tsp salt

70 g butter, at room temperature

140 g granulated sugar

Reactivate your starter the day before you plan on building the levain. A good time to do this is when you get up in the morning, to allow the starter 6 to 8 hours to become bubbly and active. You will need 25 grams for the levain and at least 20 grams for maintaining your original starter/main culture (see page 14 for more information on the feeding ratio).

Build the levain: Using a kitchen scale, weigh 25 grams of active starter in a clean 500-milliliter jar. Vigorously whisk in 50 grams of warm water, then add 25 grams of buckwheat flour and 25 grams of brown rice flour. Ferment the levain for 6 to 8 hours, or until it is bubbly and has risen to a peak, before mixing it into the dough.

Mix the batter: Grease a 9-inch (23-cm)-wide, 10-cup (2.5-L) Bundt® pan with olive oil. Sprinkle a thin layer of the cocoa powder over the oil. Set the pan aside. In a large bowl, combine the almond flour, sweet white rice flour, oat flour, buckwheat flour, sorghum flour, tapioca starch, baking soda, cinnamon, ginger and salt. In a medium bowl, use a handheld mixer to beat together the butter and granulated sugar for about 2 minutes, until they are smooth and creamy. Then, beat in the eggs. Add the levain and water, then sprinkle the psyllium husk and flaxseed on top of the mixture. Lightly beat the mixture to prevent lumps from forming. Stir the carrots and apple into the levain mixture. Add the carrot-apple mixture to the flour blend. Mix the batter well by hand, or with a kitchen mixer fitted with a dough hook running at medium-low speed, until all the ingredients are fully incorporated. Transfer the cake batter to the prepared Bundt pan. The batter will be about 2 inches (5 cm) from the top of the Bundt pan.

Proof: Cover the top of the Bundt pan with plastic wrap. Let the batter rest at room temperature—ideally about 72°F (22°C)—for 7 to 8 hours. The proofing time depends on the temperature of your kitchen. If the temperature is a little colder, place the Bundt pan in the oven with the light on. In the summer warmth, it can be left on the counter, and the batter may benefit from less proofing time. When the batter has proofed enough, it will have risen nearly to the top of the pan and will feel soft and spongy on top.

Cake (cont.)

3 large eggs, at room temperature

100 g water, at room temperature

10 g whole psyllium husk

4 g flaxseed, finely ground

250 g grated carrots (about 2 large carrots)

90 g peeled, thinly sliced and cooked Gala apple (1 medium apple)

Cream Cheese and Yogurt Icing

30 g butter, at room temperature

80 g powdered sugar

80 g cream cheese, at room temperature

60 g plain unsweetened full-fat Greek yogurt, at room temperature

1 tsp fresh lemon juice

Bake: Preheat the oven to 350°F (177°C). Bake the cake for 45 minutes, or until it feels firm and set on top and a toothpick inserted into the center comes out clean.

Let the cake cool in the pan for 15 to 20 minutes, then remove it and transfer it to a wire rack to cool for at least 2 hours.

Make the cream cheese and yogurt icing. Melt the butter in a small saucepan over low heat. Turn off the heat and add the powdered sugar, cream cheese, Greek yogurt and lemon juice to the butter, stirring the ingredients until there are no lumps—the icing should be smooth and easily spreadable. Spread the icing over the top of the cooled cake.

This cake is best served fresh, but it can be stored, covered, on the counter for up to 2 days.

See image on page 118.

quiche, pasties *and* pies

Pies were always one of my favorite desserts in my pre-celiac days, and it took considerable time to perfect a gluten-free pastry. Now with the addition of gluten-free sourdough, pastry has made a comeback in my house! I cannot believe how easy it is to work with this pastry and how good it tastes. It does not have the gritty, sandy texture you often get with some gluten-free baked goods.

Pastry dough can easily be made a day ahead of the actual recipe, and the fillings can also be prepared before shaping and baking the pies. The choices for fruit pies are limitless—there are so many tasty combinations. One of my favorite combinations makes an appearance in the Blackberry and Apple Pie (page 142). And my favorite savory pie is the Cornish Pasties or Hand Pies (page 145). Each recipe is unique and exceptionally good—it is hard to believe that they are all safe for a celiac diet.

Blackberry *and* Apple Pie

In my garden, there are three thornless blackberry bushes that produce copious amounts of berries that I can pick fresh and put straight into a pie. I do not always have a lot of time in a day to bake desserts, so I spread the work out by mixing the dough the day before I bake the pie, leaving the shaping and baking for the next day, so I can get a fantastic pie with minimal time and effort—there is nothing like blackberries mingling with apples, the juices oozing onto the plate!

Makes 1 (9-inch [23-cm]) pie

Levain

20 g active starter

40 g warm water

20 g buckwheat flour

20 g brown rice flour

Pie

80 g almond flour

45 g oat flour

70 g sweet white rice flour

50 g buckwheat flour

70 g brown sugar

3 g salt

1 large egg, at room temperature

100 g melted butter, cooled until warm

10 g flaxseed, finely ground

White rice flour, as needed

Reactivate your starter the day before you plan on building the levain. A good time to do this is when you get up in the morning, to allow the starter 6 to 8 hours to become bubbly and active. You will need 20 grams for the levain and at least 20 grams for maintaining your original starter/main culture (see page 14 for more information on the feeding ratio).

Build the levain: Using a kitchen scale, weigh 20 grams of active starter in a clean 500-milliliter jar. Vigorously mix in the 40 grams of warm water, then add 20 grams of buckwheat flour and 20 grams of brown rice flour. Ferment the levain for 6 to 8 hours, or until it is bubbly and has risen to a peak, before mixing it into the dough.

Mix the dough: In a large bowl, combine the almond flour, oat flour, sweet white rice flour, buckwheat flour, brown sugar and salt. In a medium bowl, use a handheld mixer to beat the egg, then add the butter and flaxseed. Add the levain to the egg mixture and beat lightly to combine the ingredients. Add the levain mixture to the flour blend. Using your hands, knead the dough in the bowl for 2 to 3 minutes, until all the flour is well combined. Form the dough into a ball.

Ferment: Place the dough in a 4-cup (1-L) proofing bowl, cover it with a lid and let it rest in a warm location for 30 to 60 minutes, or until it feels soft on top and has risen a little. Place the covered dough in the fridge for 1 to 2 hours, or overnight.

(continued)

Blackberry *and* Apple Pie (continued)

Filling

300 g fresh or thawed frozen blackberries

200 g peeled and thinly sliced Gala apples (2 medium apples)

60 g brown sugar

30 g cornstarch

Toppings

150 g fresh or thawed frozen blackberries

200 g peeled and thinly sliced Gala apples (2 medium apples)

20 g granulated sugar

Prepare the filling: Remove the dough from the fridge and let it rest at room temperature while you prepare the filling. In a medium pot over medium heat, combine the blackberries, apples, brown sugar and cornstarch. Cook the ingredients for about 5 minutes, stirring them frequently, just until the mixture thickens. Set the filling aside to cool while you proceed with the next steps.

Shape: Cut two 11-inch (28-cm) circles of parchment paper. Set the parchment paper circles aside. Cut the dough in half. Place each piece of dough on a parchment paper circle. Dust the surface of the first piece of dough with the white rice flour. Roll out the first piece of dough, which will become the bottom crust, until it is 11 inches (28 cm) in diameter. Repeat this process with the second piece of dough to create the top crust. Transfer both pieces of dough, still on the parchment paper circles, to the refrigerator to chill for 10 to 15 minutes.

Remove the bottom crust from the fridge. Carefully place the bottom crust upside down into a 9-inch (23-cm) pie plate and remove the parchment paper from the dough.

Bake: Preheat the oven to 400°F (204°C). Bake the bottom crust for 6 minutes. Add the cooked filling, then top the filling with the blackberries, apples and granulated sugar. Remove the top crust from the fridge and place it over the pie. Seal and trim the pastry edges. Cut vents in the top of the pastry to let the steam escape, but if you are creating a lattice pastry top, then this is not necessary. Reduce the oven's temperature to 375°F (191°C) for 15 to 20 minutes. If the pie is browning too quickly, cover it with aluminum foil. Reduce the oven's temperature to 350°F (177°C) and bake the pie for 12 to 15 minutes, until the crust is golden brown.

Let the pie cool for about 15 minutes before slicing it.

Serve the pie while it is still warm. You can also cover the pie plate with plastic wrap and store the pie in the fridge if you have leftovers for the next day.

Cornish Pasties *or* Hand Pies

Here is a flaky gluten-free pastry with no fuss! Just throw all the ingredients into a bowl, mix them together and chill the dough in the fridge. This dough rolls out brilliantly, and there is no comparison to store-bought pastry. Grab a pastie, then add a green salad and perhaps a gluten-free beer for a marvelous meal. This sort of food reminds me of my pre-celiac days in New Zealand, and sometimes it is the small things in life that make me happy. Recipe inspiration by my brother David!

Makes 6 hand pies

Levain

30 g active starter
60 g warm water
30 g buckwheat flour
30 g brown rice flour

Pasties or Pies

40 g oat flour
120 g boiling water
70 g sorghum flour
60 g brown rice flour
60 g potato starch
8 g salt
¼ tsp black pepper
1 large egg, at room temperature
15 g warm water
10 g whole psyllium husk
80 g cold butter, grated
White rice flour, as needed

Reactivate your starter the day before you plan on building the levain. A good time to do this is when you get up in the morning, to allow the starter 6 to 8 hours to become bubbly and active. You will need 30 grams for the levain and at least 20 grams for maintaining your original starter/main culture (see page 14 for more information on the feeding ratio).

Build the levain: Using a kitchen scale, weigh 30 grams of active starter in a clean 500-milliliter jar. Vigorously mix in 60 grams of warm water, then add 30 grams of buckwheat flour and 30 grams of brown rice flour. Ferment the levain for 6 to 8 hours, or until it is bubbly and has risen to a peak, before mixing it into the dough.

Mix the dough: Place the oat flour in a medium saucepan, and pour in the boiling water. Immediately whisk the oat flour and water until they form a smooth paste, mashing any lumps. Leave the paste to cool for about 10 minutes, or until it is just warm to the touch. In a large bowl, combine the sorghum flour, brown rice flour, potato starch, salt and black pepper. Add the egg and levain to the cooled oat paste, beating the ingredients to combine them. Add the warm water, and then stir in the psyllium husk to make a gel. Immediately whisk the mixture to prevent lumps from forming. Add the levain-psyllium mixture to the flour blend. Mix the dough well by hand, or with a kitchen mixer fitted with a dough hook running at medium-low speed, until all the ingredients are fully incorporated. Add the butter to the dough and mix it in with your fingertips to evenly incorporate it.

Ferment: Place the dough in a 4-cup (1-L) proofing bowl, cover it with a lid and let it rest in a warm location for 30 to 60 minutes. It will puff up a little. Place the covered dough in the fridge for 1 to 2 hours, or overnight.

(continued)

Cornish Pasties *or* Hand Pies (continued)

Filling

400 g ground beef or cooked lentils

½ diced medium onion

1 diced large carrot

1 tsp salt

¼ tsp black pepper

180 g hot water

1 beef or vegetable bouillon cube

1 tsp soy sauce

7 g cornstarch

1 tsp cold water

100 g diced russet potato

Egg Wash

1 large cold egg

15 g cool water

Filling: Remove the pastry dough from the fridge. In a medium skillet over medium heat, cook the beef for about 5 minutes, until it is lightly browned (if you are using cooked lentils, skip this step and begin by cooking the onion, carrot, salt and black pepper over medium heat). Add the onion, carrot, salt and black pepper and cook the mixture for about 10 minutes, or until the vegetables begin to soften. Add the hot water, bouillon cube and soy sauce, and stir the mixture to dissolve the bouillon cube. In a small cup, make a paste by combining the cornstarch and cold water. Stir this paste into the mixture in the skillet. Add the potato and cook the filling for 1 minute, until it begins to thicken a little. Cover the skillet, reduce the heat to medium-low and cook the filling for 10 minutes. Remove the skillet from the heat and chill the filling in the fridge for 20 minutes, or until it is cool to the touch, before adding it to the pastry.

Shape: Cut six 8-inch (20-cm) circles of parchment paper and lay them on a work surface. Next, make the egg wash. In a small bowl, beat together the egg and cool water. Set the egg wash aside.

Lightly dust a work surface with white rice flour. Transfer the dough to the prepared work surface and split it into six 100-gram pieces. On each piece of parchment paper, roll a piece of dough into a 6-inch (15-cm)-diameter circle. Place each dough circle, still on the parchment paper, on a large baking sheet. Transfer the baking sheet to the fridge and allow the dough to chill for 15 minutes. Remove the baking sheet from the fridge, then add 80 grams of the filling—about the size of a golf ball—to each dough circle. Place the filling on one side of the dough circle, fold the dough circle in half using the parchment paper and brush the egg wash on the inside edge of the dough before pinching the edges together with your fingers to seal the hand pie.

Bake: Preheat the oven to 425°F (218°C). Meanwhile, brush the tops of the hand pies with the egg wash. Place the baking sheet on the oven's middle rack and bake the hand pies for 25 minutes. Reduce the oven's temperature to 350°F (177°C) and bake the hand pies for 10 minutes, or until the pastry is light brown.

Let the hand pies cool on the baking sheet for about 15 minutes before removing them.

Serve the hand pies while they are still warm. Store any remaining hand pies, covered, in the fridge for 2 to 3 days.

Mixed-Berry Galettes

This is a taste of summer goodness packed into a crispy, gluten-free quinoa crust that is quick and easy to make. I prefer a rustic appearance to the crust. I also like to use seasonal fruits for the filling, and I enjoy eating a warm slice topped with some ice cream. Once you bite into a slice, it is "berry" hard to stop.

—✦—

Makes 2 (10-inch [25-cm]) galettes

Levain

40 g active starter
80 g warm water
40 g quinoa flour
40 g brown rice flour
5 g granulated sugar

Galettes

70 g quinoa flour
20 g sorghum flour
40 g tapioca starch
75 g brown sugar
1 tsp salt
50 g coconut oil
30 g fresh orange juice
5 g whole psyllium husk
12 g flaxseed, finely ground
White rice flour, as needed

Reactivate your starter the day before you plan on building the levain. A good time to do this is when you get up in the morning, to allow the starter 6 to 8 hours to become bubbly and active. You will need 40 grams for the levain and at least 20 grams for maintaining your original starter/main culture (see page 14 for more information on the feeding ratio).

Build the levain: Using a kitchen scale, weigh 40 grams of active starter in a clean 500-milliliter jar. Vigorously whisk in 80 grams of warm water, then add 40 grams of quinoa flour, 40 grams of brown rice flour and 5 grams of granulated sugar. Ferment the levain for 6 to 8 hours, or until it is bubbly and has risen to a peak, before mixing it into the dough.

Mix the dough: In a large bowl, combine the quinoa flour, sorghum flour, tapioca starch, brown sugar and salt. Melt the coconut oil in a small saucepan over medium-low heat, then remove it from the heat and allow it to cool until it is lukewarm. Add the orange juice to the coconut oil. Stir the psyllium husk and flaxseed into the coconut oil mixture and immediately whisk the ingredients to prevent lumps from forming. Stir the levain into the coconut oil mixture, and then add the oil-levain mixture to the flour blend. Mix the dough well by hand, or with a kitchen mixer fitted with a dough hook running at medium-low speed, until all the ingredients are fully incorporated.

Ferment: Form the dough into a ball, then place it in a 4-cup (1-L) proofing bowl. Cover the bowl with its lid and let the dough rest in a warm location for 2 or 3 hours, until it just begins to rise and feel lighter to the touch.

Shape: Cut two 12-inch (30-cm) circles of parchment paper and set them aside. Lightly dust a work surface with the white rice flour. Transfer the dough to the prepared surface. Cut the dough in half, then use a kitchen scale to make sure each piece weighs 250 grams. Place each half of dough on a parchment paper circle. Roll out each piece of dough until it is 10 inches (25 cm) in diameter. Chill the dough, still on the parchment paper, in the refrigerator while you prepare the filling.

(continued)

Mixed-Berry Galettes (continued)

Filling

7 g cornstarch

15 g cold water

200 g fresh or frozen
blueberries, at room
temperature

100 g fresh or frozen
strawberries, at room
temperature

40 g granulated sugar

100 g unpeeled grated Gala
apple (1 medium apple)

1 tsp fresh lemon juice

Filling: In a medium pot, combine the cornstarch and cold water, stirring them to make a paste. Add the blueberries, strawberries and granulated sugar. Cook this mixture over medium heat for about 5 minutes, stirring it continuously, until it has thickened. Stir in the apple and lemon juice and cook the filling for 1 minute. Set the filling aside to cool until it is lukewarm.

Bake: Preheat the oven to 425°F (218°C). Meanwhile, carefully slide the parchment paper with the dough onto a large baking sheet. Divide the filling evenly between the two pieces of dough. Fold and crimp the edges of the dough to contain the filling. Bake the galettes on the oven's middle rack for 20 minutes. Reduce the oven's temperature to 350°F (177°C) and bake the galettes for 10 minutes, until their crusts are crispy and light brown. If you find that the crusts are browning too quickly, cover them with tented aluminum foil.

Transfer the parchment paper with the galettes to a wire rack. Let the galettes cool for 20 minutes before serving them.

These galettes are best while still warm, but they will keep, covered, in the fridge for 3 to 4 days. Reheat leftovers in the oven at 350°F (177°C) for 10 minutes.

Sourdough Quiche

This is a delicious quiche, or open-faced pie, with a light and flaky crust. The oils from the pumpkin seeds in this gluten-free pie crust reduce the fat content without compromising the texture and taste. Mix and place the dough in a tart pan, leave it in the refrigerator overnight and bake it the next day. This dish is ideal for lunch, dinner or a picnic. This recipe is flexible, so you can adjust it to your individual taste by replacing filling ingredients—try swapping the broccoli with asparagus, peppers or other vegetables.

Makes 8 servings

Levain

25 g active starter

50 g warm water

25 g buckwheat flour

25 g brown rice flour

Quiche

50 g ground raw unsalted pumpkin seeds

25 g buckwheat flour

35 g brown rice flour

40 g sorghum flour

25 g quinoa flour

50 g potato starch

1 tsp salt

¼ tsp black pepper

60 g plain, unsweetened full-fat Greek yogurt, at room temperature

70 g grated butter, at room temperature

70 g warm water

7 g whole psyllium husk

White rice flour, as needed

Reactivate your starter the day before you plan on building the levain. A good time to do this is when you get up in the morning, to allow the starter 6 to 8 hours to become bubbly and active. You will need 25 grams for the levain and at least 20 grams for maintaining your original starter/main culture (see page 14 for more information on the feeding ratio).

Build the levain: Using a kitchen scale, weigh 25 grams of active starter in a clean 500-milliliter jar. Vigorously mix in 50 grams of warm water, then add 25 grams of buckwheat flour and 25 grams of brown rice flour. Ferment the levain for 6 to 8 hours, or until it is bubbly and has risen to a peak, before mixing it into the dough.

Mix the dough: In a small food processor, grind the pumpkin seeds into flour. Line the bottom of a 8 x 5 x 4–inch (20 x 13 x 10–cm) rectangular tart pan or a 9-inch (23-cm) pie plate with parchment paper. In a large bowl, combine the buckwheat flour, brown rice flour, sorghum flour, quinoa flour, potato starch, salt, black pepper and pumpkin seed flour. In a medium bowl, combine the Greek yogurt, butter and warm water. Stir in the psyllium husk and whisk the ingredients immediately to prevent lumps from forming. Mix in the levain. Add the yogurt mixture to the flour blend. Mix the dough well by hand, or with a kitchen mixer fitted with a dough hook running at medium-low speed, until all the ingredients are fully incorporated.

Ferment: Lightly dust a work surface with the white rice flour. Place a large piece of parchment paper next to the prepared work surface. Transfer the dough to the prepared work surface. Knead the dough for 2 to 3 minutes. Transfer the dough to the parchment paper and roll the dough out to fit the prepared tart pan. Carefully place the dough in the prepared tart pan. Cover the tart pan with plastic wrap and let the dough rest in a warm location for 30 to 60 minutes, until the dough begins to rise. Place the covered dough in the fridge for the night. Alternatively, you can leave the dough on the counter to rise for 2 to 3 hours and then chill it in the fridge for 30 minutes before baking it.

(continued)

Sourdough Quiche (continued)

Filling

3 to 4 slices bacon

4 large cold eggs

80 g cold milk

½ medium onion, thinly sliced

1 large tomato, thinly sliced

60 g grated Cheddar cheese

2 medium crowns broccoli, finely chopped

6 g fresh chives or green onions (green parts only), finely chopped

8 g salt

¼ tsp black pepper

Filling: The next day, remove the dough from the fridge and take off the plastic wrap. Preheat the oven to 400°F (204°C). With a fork, prick holes in the bottom of the crust and bake the empty crust for 10 minutes. This will prevent the crust from absorbing too much moisture from the filling. Meanwhile, in a small skillet over medium-high heat, cook the bacon for 6 to 8 minutes, until it is crispy. Remove the skillet from the heat. In a medium bowl, lightly beat the eggs and cold milk together. Stir in the bacon, onion (reserving a few slices for the top of the quiche), tomato (reserving a few slices for the top of the quiche), Cheddar cheese, broccoli, chives, salt and black pepper. Pour the filling into the crust, then arrange the onion slices and tomato slices on top of the filling.

Bake: Reduce the oven's temperature to 375°F (191°C). Bake the quiche for 30 minutes, or until the filling feels firm on top and a toothpick inserted into the center comes out clean.

Let the quiche cool on a wire rack for about 15 minutes before removing it from the tart pan. Serve the quiche warm right away. Store any leftovers, covered, in the fridge for 2 to 3 days.

leftover *sourdough* starter treats

When you bake with sourdough, you have a starter that is fed daily with flour and water, which soon outgrows your jar—this means you need to discard some starter at every feed. You can bake something small with the excess starter each day, but usually it is easier to place it in one dedicated sourdough discard jar in the fridge. When the jar starts to get full, you can make a batch of Garlic Naan (page 160) or any of the other leftover sourdough starter recipes in this chapter. Please note that the discard in the fridge will continue to sour, and after three or four weeks it can become too pungent and sour to use, even for the Tasty Cheese Crackers (page 168). So, bake up before then!

Carrot Tortillas

Carrot tortillas make the best taco shells, and you can load on more garden-fresh vegetables for a satisfying and healthy meal. You cannot compare these to store-bought gluten-free tortillas—the flavor and texture of these tortillas are far superior, with the binding properties and the slight tanginess from the starter. I make these tortillas on my days off, and they are one of my favorite lunches for workdays. It's easy to change up the fillings for some variety. These will not fall apart when you pick them up, as most other gluten-free tortillas do.

—✦—

Makes 7 tortillas

150 g grated carrot (2 medium carrots)

30 g warm water

80 g grated Cheddar cheese

¼ tsp curry powder

7 g flaxseed, finely ground

5 g salt

2 large eggs, at room temperature

180 g leftover active starter, at room temperature and no more than 1 week old

40 g potato starch

20 g sorghum flour

Mix the dough: Place the carrot and warm water in a medium saucepan. Cover the saucepan with its lid and cook the carrot over medium-high heat for 3 minutes. Remove the lid, increase the heat to high and cook the carrot for 1 minute, stirring it constantly, until the water has evaporated. Turn off the heat and leave the carrot in the saucepan to cool for 5 minutes. Mix in the Cheddar cheese, curry powder, flaxseed and salt. In a medium bowl, beat together the eggs and leftover active starter. Add the egg-starter mixture to the carrot mixture, then mix in the potato starch and sorghum flour.

Ferment: Transfer the dough to a 4-cup (1-L) proofing bowl. Cover the bowl with its lid and let the dough rest on the counter for 30 minutes. In the meantime, line two large baking sheets with parchment paper.

Shape: Using a ⅓-cup (80-g) measuring cup, scoop out some of the dough and evenly spread it into a 6-inch (15-cm) circle that is about ¼ inch (6 mm) thick on one of the prepared baking sheets. Use the bottom of the measuring cup to smooth out the top of the tortilla. Repeat this procedure to create seven tortillas. The thinner the tortillas are, the crispier they will become.

Bake: Preheat the oven to 400°F (204°C). Bake the tortillas for 18 to 20 minutes, rotating the baking sheets after 10 minutes, until the tortillas are crispy on the edges.

Gently remove the carrot tortillas from the baking sheets while they are still warm and transfer them to a taco rack. If you do not have a taco rack, you can create a taco shape by curving the tortillas around a small bottle. Let the tortillas cool completely.

Store the tortillas, stacked together and covered in beeswax wraps or a tea towel, on the counter for up to 2 days. After 2 days, keep them, covered, in the fridge for up to 1 week.

Garden Vegetable Flatbread

This garlic-infused, thin, crispy bread makes a flavorsome appetizer or snack. This flatbread is an excellent way to use up discarded starter that may have been sitting around too long, might be past its peak or may have been sitting in your discard jar for a couple of weeks. You can be creative and arrange fresh, seasonal garden vegetables on the top of the dough to make your own masterpiece.

—⊀—

Makes 1 Flatbread

Flatbread

300 g cold leftover active starter, no more than 2 weeks old

60 g warm water

30 g olive oil

10 g whole psyllium husk

30 g millet flour

35 g buckwheat flour

25 g potato starch

½ tsp baking powder

9 g salt

2 cloves garlic, minced

Toppings

15 g olive oil

3 g fresh rosemary, thyme or basil, finely chopped

3 or 4 thin spears asparagus, tough ends removed

¼ medium zucchini, thinly sliced

1 green onion, finely chopped

¼ medium red onion, sliced into small, thin rings

¼ red bell pepper, thinly sliced

½ tsp salt

½ tsp black pepper

Mix the dough: Place the leftover active starter in a medium bowl. Pour in the warm water and olive oil, and then sprinkle the psyllium husk on top. Whisk this mixture immediately to prevent lumps from forming. Add the millet flour, buckwheat flour, potato starch, baking powder and salt. Mix the dough well by hand, or with a kitchen mixer fitted with a dough hook running at medium-low speed, until all the ingredients are fully incorporated. Mix in the garlic.

Ferment: Form the dough into a ball, then place it in a 4-cup (1-L) proofing bowl. Cover the bowl with its lid and let the dough rest on the counter for 3 to 4 hours, until it looks slightly puffy. Do not expect this dough to rise much.

Shape: Cut a 12 x 10–inch (30 x 25–cm) piece of parchment paper, and place it on a large pizza stone. On the parchment paper, roll out the dough until it is about ½ inch (1.3 cm) thick. Now, it's time to top the flatbread. Spread the olive oil over the top of the dough and add the herbs, asparagus, zucchini, green onion, red onion, bell pepper, salt and black pepper. If you like, you can create a design with the toppings.

Bake: Preheat the oven to 425°F (218°C). Bake the flatbread for 35 minutes, or until the vegetables are roasted and the dough is golden brown and crispy.

Place the flatbread on a wire rack to cool for 20 minutes before serving it.

This flatbread is best eaten while it is still warm. Store any leftover flatbread, covered in beeswax wraps or plastic wrap, on a plate in the fridge for up to 24 hours.

Garlic Naan

Buttery, garlicky homemade naan bread is the best thing ever! Naan is a flatbread usually made with yeast, but it is spectacular with the addition of sourdough instead. You are missing out if you do not give this recipe a try. Who needs cutlery when you can scoop up all the goodness on your plate with a chunk of this bread?

Makes 9 naans

Naan

125 g warm water

80 g plain, unsweetened full-fat Greek yogurt, at room temperature

160 g leftover active starter, at room temperature and 1 to 2 days old

8 g whole psyllium husk

15 g melted butter, cooled until lukewarm

35 g sorghum flour

50 g brown rice flour

15 g tapioca starch

1 to 2 cloves garlic, crushed

White rice flour, as needed

15 g avocado or vegetable oil, plus more as needed

Cool water, as needed

Herbed Garlic Butter

50 g butter, softened

2 cloves garlic, minced

10 g finely chopped fresh parsley

¼ tsp salt

Mix the dough: In a medium bowl, stir together the warm water and Greek yogurt. Add the leftover active starter and psyllium husk. Whisk the mixture immediately to prevent lumps from forming. Stir in the butter, sorghum flour, brown rice flour, tapioca starch and garlic.

Ferment: Form the dough into a ball, then place it in a 4-cup (1-L) proofing bowl. Cover the bowl with its lid and leave the dough on the counter to rest for 30 minutes.

Shape: Lightly dust a work surface with the white rice flour. Transfer the dough to the prepared work surface. Knead the dough for 2 to 3 minutes, then use a bench scraper or knife to cut the dough into nine equal pieces, about 48 g each. Shape each piece of dough into a rough disk, about 5 inches (13 cm) in diameter.

Proof: Line a large baking sheet with parchment paper. Transfer the dough disks to the prepared baking sheet. Cover the dough with a damp tea towel and let it rise for about 2 hours, until it has risen slightly and is puffy.

Steam the naan: Heat the avocado oil in a medium cast-iron skillet over medium-high heat. Place a dough disk into the hot skillet, add a few drops of the cool water and immediately cover the skillet with its lid to steam the naan, being careful not to burn yourself. Reduce the heat to medium and cook each side of the naan for 2 to 4 minutes, until the naan has puffed up slightly and is lightly browned. Repeat this process with the remaining dough disks, adding enough additional avocado oil to the skillet to lightly coat the bottom if it becomes too dry. Keep the cooked naans in the oven at its lowest temperature setting while the others cook.

Prepare the herbed garlic butter: In a small bowl, combine the butter, garlic, parsley and salt.

Serve the naans with the herbed garlic butter.

These are best eaten warm the day they are made. Store any leftovers, covered with beeswax wraps or in a tea towel, for up to 24 hours.

Herbed Bread Sticks

These simple yet superb bread sticks pair wonderfully with a charcuterie board, and they make a great side to a steaming bowl of soup. Gather the sourdough discard from your fridge, mix up the dough and let it sit in your fridge for a day or two before shaping—or, if you just can't wait, you can bake the bread sticks the same day you mix the dough. Eat these hot from the oven or after they've cooled.

⟶ ⟵

Makes 14 bread sticks

Bread Sticks

30 g buckwheat flour

30 g millet flour

20 g quinoa flour

40 g potato starch or tapioca starch

5 g granulated sugar

5 g salt

160 g leftover active starter, at room temperature and no more than 1 week old

60 g plain, unsweetened full-fat Greek yogurt, at room temperature

85 g warm water

10 g whole psyllium husk

20 g cold butter, grated

White rice flour, as needed

Topping

15 g olive oil

1 tsp Italian seasoning

1 tsp salt

Mix the dough: In a medium bowl, combine the buckwheat flour, millet flour, quinoa flour, potato starch, sugar and salt. In another medium bowl, combine the leftover active starter and Greek yogurt, and then stir in the warm water. Stir the psyllium husk into the starter mix and immediately whisk the mixture to prevent lumps from forming. Add the wet mixture to the flour and add in the butter, mixing it with your hands to incorporate it well.

Ferment: Form the dough into a ball, then place it in a 4-cup (1-L) proofing bowl. Cover the bowl with its lid and leave the dough on the counter to rest for 30 to 60 minutes, or until it feels slightly soft and spongy.

Shape: Place a piece of parchment paper on top of a large pizza stone or baking sheet. Lightly dust a work surface with the white rice flour. Transfer the dough to the prepared work surface. Knead the dough for 2 to 3 minutes, and then roll it out into an 11 x 8–inch (28 x 20–cm) rectangle. Cut the dough across the short side into 14 fingers that are 8 inches (20 cm) long and slightly wider than an adult finger. Turn and gently twist the dough about three times to create a spiral look without adding extra length and making the bread sticks too thin. To top the bread sticks, brush the oil on the top of each bread stick, then sprinkle the Italian seasoning and salt on each one.

Bake: Preheat the oven 400°F (204°C). Bake the bread sticks for 25 to 30 minutes, until they are golden brown and have a crispy crust.

Transfer the bread sticks to a wire rack and allow them to cool for about 5 minutes. Serve them while they are still warm. They are also good cold and will keep, covered in beeswax wraps or a tea towel, on the counter for up to 2 days.

The Best Pancakes *and* Waffles

These fluffy, gluten-free pancakes or waffles are delicious topped with your favorite syrup, sauces or fresh fruit. Using sourdough in this simple recipe creates a soft and light center with that crispy outer layer you'll love. These are so easy to make the night before—then all you have to do is cook them in the morning. Refrigerate any remaining batter in a sealed jar, and it will keep for up to 2 days. For a thicker batter, add a little less water; for a thinner consistency, add a little more water.

Makes 7 pancakes or waffles

200 g leftover active starter, preferably 1 to 2 days old

100 g milk, at room temperature

20 g olive oil

2 large eggs, at room temperature

8 g granulated sugar

5 g flaxseed, finely ground

30 g buckwheat flour

35 g millet flour

20 g tapioca starch

½ tsp baking powder

⅛ tsp salt

15 to 30 g avocado or vegetable oil

Mix the dough: In a medium bowl, beat together the leftover active starter, milk, olive oil, eggs and sugar for about 1 minute. Stir in the flaxseed and beat the ingredients again, until they are just combined. Stir in the buckwheat flour, millet flour, tapioca starch, baking powder and salt until the ingredients are just combined.

Ferment: Cover the bowl and leave the batter in the fridge overnight for a quick and easy batch of pancakes the next morning. Alternatively, allow the batter to rest on the counter for 30 to 40 minutes. The batter may look a little bubbly, but don't worry if it does not.

Make the pancakes: To make pancakes, lightly coat the bottom of a medium skillet with the avocado oil. Place the skillet over medium-high heat. Scoop about ⅓ cup (80 g) of batter into the skillet and cook the pancake for 2 to 3 minutes, until bubbles poke through the top of the batter. Flip the pancake over and cook it for 1 or 2 minutes, until the pancake is light brown. Repeat the process with the remaining batter.

Make the waffles: Preheat a waffle maker. Scoop ⅓ cup (80 g) of batter into the waffle maker and cook the waffle for 3 to 5 minutes, depending on the manufacturer's instructions. Keep a close eye on the waffle and remove it when it is light brown and no longer wet on the inside.

Serve the pancakes or waffles while they are still warm. Store any leftovers, covered with a beeswax wrap or tea towel, on the counter for 24 hours.

Seeded Teff Crackers

There is always spare starter discard in my fridge, but if you find you do not have much, it is worthwhile to feed your starter just to make these delicious crackers. With pumpkin seeds, sesame seeds, sunflower seeds and a touch of cayenne pepper, these crispy crackers make a flavorful and healthy snack.

I always look for raw, unseasoned seeds and nuts because they are usually gluten-free. Always check the ingredients list to make sure.

Makes about 50 crackers

250 g cold leftover active starter, no more than 2 weeks old

30 g honey or pure maple syrup

40 g olive oil

35 g teff flour

10 g buckwheat flour

12 g finely ground flaxseed

15 g hemp seeds

15 g sesame seeds

30 g roughly chopped raw unsalted sunflower seeds

30 g roughly chopped raw unsalted pumpkin seeds

1 tsp salt-free garlic and herb seasoning

4 g salt

½ tsp cayenne pepper or chipotle seasoning

¼ tsp black pepper

White rice flour, as needed

1 tsp sesame seeds

Mix the dough: In a medium bowl, whisk together the leftover active starter, honey and olive oil. Add the teff flour and buckwheat flour, then add the flaxseed, hemp seeds, sesame seeds, sunflower seeds, pumpkin seeds, garlic and herb seasoning, salt, cayenne pepper and black pepper. Combine the ingredients well.

Ferment: Form the dough into a ball, then place it in a 4-cup (1-L) proofing bowl. Cover the bowl with its lid and leave the dough to rest on the counter for 1 to 2 hours, or overnight.

Shape: Line a large baking sheet with parchment paper, then dust the parchment paper with the white rice flour. Lightly dust a work surface with the white rice flour. Transfer the dough to the prepared work surface and roll the dough into a small square. Place the square of dough on the prepared baking sheet and roll it into a 14 x 14–inch (35 x 35–cm) square. With a pastry cutter or knife, cut all the way through the dough to create 2 x 2–inch (5 x 5–cm) squares. Evenly sprinkle the sesame seeds over the top of the dough.

Bake: Preheat the oven to 300°F (149°C). Place the baking sheet on the oven's middle rack and bake the crackers for 45 minutes, or until they are light golden brown in color and the edges are crispy. Turn off the oven and let the crackers sit in the oven to cool for 15 minutes. Transfer the crackers to a wire rack to finish cooling.

Store the crackers in an airtight container for up to 1 week.

Tasty Cheese Crackers

Another great solution for using up your sourdough discard is to make these cheesy, crispy, salted crackers. These are so quick and easy to make, but I must warn you that they can also be addictive! The thinner you roll them, the crispier they will be. These crackers are perfect for snacking or enjoying with a bowl of tomato soup.

Makes about 80 crackers

400 g leftover active starter, no more than 2 weeks old

35 g olive oil

30 g warm water

5 g flaxseed, finely ground

75 g buckwheat flour

25 g sorghum flour

50 g tapioca starch

30 g sweet white rice flour

1 tsp salt

6 g fresh rosemary, finely chopped

⅛ tsp black pepper

80 g grated sharp Cheddar cheese

White rice flour, as needed

Mix the dough: In a medium bowl, whisk together the leftover active starter, olive oil, warm water and flaxseed. In another medium bowl, combine the buckwheat flour, sorghum flour, tapioca starch, sweet white rice flour, salt, rosemary and black pepper. Add the starter mixture to the flour, mix the ingredients well and then stir in the Cheddar cheese.

Ferment: Form the dough into a ball, then place it in a 4-cup (1-L) proofing bowl. Cover the bowl with its lid and leave the dough to rest on the counter for 30 minutes, until it is soft to the touch and a little puffy. The appearance will not change much.

Shape: Cut a piece of parchment paper to fit a large baking sheet, then dust the parchment paper with the white rice flour. Place the dough on the prepared parchment paper and roll the dough out into a square that is ¼ inch (6 mm) thick. Carefully transfer the dough, still on the parchment paper, to the large baking sheet. With a pastry cutter or knife, cut all the way through the dough to create 2 x 2–inch (5 x 5–cm) squares.

Bake: Preheat the oven to 375°F (191°C). Place the baking sheet on the oven's middle rack and bake the crackers for 25 minutes. Reduce the oven's temperature to 325°F (163°C) and bake the crackers for 15 to 20 minutes, until they are light and crispy and golden brown in color.

Transfer the crackers to a wire rack to cool completely.

Store the crackers in an airtight container for up to 1 week.

Cauliflower Pizza Crust

The flavorful, crispy goodness of cauliflower pizza crust is still popular, and this gluten-free version will not disappoint. It bakes up scrumptious with crunchy edges and is loaded with that extra serving of vegetables from the cauliflower. One of best things about this gluten-free crust is that you can pick it up and hold it in your hands—it will not droop like many other types of gluten-free crusts. Store the dough in an airtight container in the fridge for up to two days if you do not want to use it right away.

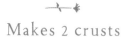

Makes 2 crusts

Starter

40 g leftover active starter, at room temperature and 1 to 2 days old

40 g warm water

20 g brown rice flour

20 g buckwheat flour

Cauliflower

75 g warm water

1 tsp salt

360 g cauliflower florets

10 g nutritional yeast

Pizza Crust

20 g sweet white rice flour

40 g buckwheat flour

40 g millet flour

30 g potato starch or cornstarch

9 g salt

70 g warm water

1 large egg, at room temperature

8 g whole psyllium husk

1 tsp dried marjoram

Feed the starter discard: In a proofing bowl, mix together the leftover active starter, warm water, brown rice flour and buckwheat flour. Combine the ingredients well and let the mixture rest on the counter for 1 to 2 hours, until it has grown slightly and has some small bubbles.

Steam and process the cauliflower: This step can be done the same day or the night before you make the pizza crusts. In a medium saucepan over medium heat, combine the warm water and salt. Bring the water to a boil, add the cauliflower and cover the saucepan with its lid. Cook the cauliflower for 10 minutes, or until it is tender but not mushy. Drain the cauliflower extremely well, then transfer it to a small food processor. Add the nutritional yeast, and then process the cauliflower until it resembles bread crumbs.

Mix the pizza dough: In a large bowl, combine the sweet white rice flour, buckwheat flour, millet flour, potato starch and salt. In a medium bowl, combine the warm water and egg, and then stir in the psyllium husk. Whisk this mixture immediately to prevent lumps from forming. Whisk in the starter mixture, and then mix in the cauliflower and the marjoram. Add the cauliflower mixture into the flour blend. Mix the dough well by hand, or with a kitchen mixer fitted with a dough hook running at medium-low speed, until all the ingredients are fully incorporated.

Ferment: Form the dough into a ball, then place it in a 4-cup (1-L) proofing bowl. Cover the bowl with its lid and let the dough rest on the counter for 30 to 60 minutes, or until the dough begins to rise a little. Then, place the bowl in the fridge for the night. Alternatively, you can omit the overnight rest and shape the dough after it has rested at room temperature for about 1 hour, or until it feels slightly soft and spongy and rises a little.

White rice flour, as needed

Pizza toppings of choice

Shape: Cut two circles of parchment paper that are 11 inches (28 cm) in diameter. Dust each piece of parchment with the white rice flour. Cut the dough into two 325-gram pieces. Roll out each piece of dough on top of the parchment paper using a little white rice flour. Finish rounding and shaping the edges of the dough with wet hands.

Proof: Cover the dough with plastic wrap or a damp tea towel and let it rest at room temperature for about 2 hours. Add your favorite pizza toppings. I like to top my pizza with pizza sauce, mozzarella cheese, sliced tomatoes, bell peppers and arugula or basil.

Bake: Preheat the oven at 425°F (218°C) with two medium pizza stones or cast-iron skillets set on the middle rack. Carefully transfer the pizzas, still on the parchment paper, to the preheated pizza stones. Place one pizza on the oven's middle rack and the other pizza on the lower rack. Bake the pizzas for 25 minutes, until the crust is golden brown and the toppings are cooked to your liking, rotating them halfway through the baking time.

Let the pizzas cool on the pizza stones for 10 to 15 minutes before serving them.

This pizza is best eaten the same day, but leftovers can be stored, covered in beeswax wraps or plastic wrap, in the fridge for up to 24 hours.

See image on page 154.

Acknowledgments

Thank you to the special people in my life: To my two daughters, Steph and Sam, for the never-ending support and advice. To my husband, Doug, for putting up with a messy house and kitchen, with flour all over the place for months on end. To my friend Anna for her proofreading skills and support. To my blog readers and amazing and supportive Instagram friends.

Thank you to Anita's Organic Mill™ for supplying me with the best gluten-free flours for much of my baking.

Finally, thank you to the team at Page Street Publishing—especially Jenna, Sarah and Meg—for the easy discussions and kind words during the creation of this book.

I thank each one of you from the bottom of my heart!

About the Author

Mary Thompson is a self-taught gluten-free sourdough baker, food blogger and photographer. Mary's blog, acoupleofceliacs.com, shares many of her favorite gluten-free recipes and was created to keep a written record of family recipes that Mary converted to be safe for people with celiac disease, gluten intolerance and other health issues. Mary's gluten-free sourdough recipes have been featured on the Jillian Harris blog, Anita's Organic Mill blog and on Mary's Instagram account, @acoupleofceliacs.

Mary was born and raised in rural New Zealand with her two brothers and two sisters on a sheep and cattle farm. Her mother cooked amazing meals that were straight from the farm to the table, and she passed along her love of home-cooking to her children. Although they did not live an entirely self-sufficient lifestyle, a huge proportion of their food was from the farm.

In her early twenties, Mary left New Zealand for her first overseas trip to Europe. She continued to travel to many parts of the world before traveling to Canada. It was in the Yukon, while working at a gold mine, that Mary met her future husband. After traveling between New Zealand and Canada for a few years, the couple settled in Kelowna, where they currently reside with their two daughters and four grandchildren.

Index